ITALIAN STYLE

ITALIA

CLARKSON N. POTTER,
INC. / PUBLISHERS

DISTRIBUTED BY
CROWN PUBLISHERS,
INC. NEW YORK

N STYLE

CATHERINE SABINO
& ANGELO TONDINI

PHOTOGRAPHS BY GUY BOUCHET

DESIGN BY LOUISE FILI

SPECIAL CONSULTANT: LUCIA DONIZETTI

TO JOSEPH AND FRANCES PHELAN SABINO,
ANTONELLO AND GIUSEPPINA TONDINI

Published by Clarkson N. Potter, Inc.,
One Park Avenue, New York, New
York 10016, and simultaneously in
Canada by General Publishing Com-
pany Limited

Manufactured in Japan

Clarkson N. Potter, Potter, and
colophon are trademarks of Crown
Publishers, Inc.

Library of Congress Cataloging in
Publication Data

Sabino, Catherine.
    Italian style.
    Includes index.
    1. Interior decoration—Italy.
I. Tondini, Angelo.   II. Title.
NK2052.A1S23   1985   747.25
84-16017
ISBN 0-517-54614-0
10 9 8 7 6 5 4 3 2 1
First Edition

ACKNOWLEDGMENTS

The process of completing *Italian Style* has been many things—fun, exhausting, frustrating, and exciting. While the book had a leisurely start, it did allow us the time to speak to many people about the project, whose ideas, encouragement, and enthusiasm have been appreciated in a way we will never fully be able to express.

Our sincerest thanks to three of *Italian Style*'s biggest supporters—our agents Gayle Benderoff and Deborah Geltman who helped shape our original thoughts into a concrete proposal, who saw us through the times when the project seemed more than overwhelming—impossible—and to Nancy Novogrod for her unwavering faith in the book, her standards of excellence, which pushed us always to do more than we thought we could. To Carol Southern and Michael Fragnito for readily giving us the extra time we needed to finish the book. To Louise Fili for her tasteful art direction and Gael Dillon whose thoughts and recommendations were invaluable. To our parents, Joseph and Frances Phelan Sabino and Antonello and Giuseppina Tondini, who would not let us give in to our doubts that the book might be a never-ending project. To Guy Bouchet for his beautiful photographs and for enduring a work schedule that at times was relentless and extremely difficult. To Lucia Donizetti for her fine styling and knowledge of Italian furniture and to Joanna Brown for her wonderful ideas.

For their advice, comments, and suggestions we'd also like to thank: Giancarlo Alhadeff, Manlio Armellini, Peter Arnell, Gae Aulenti, Nino Azzarello, Aldo Ballo, Mario Bellini, Piero Bennati, Logan Bentley, Silvana Bernasconi, Laura Biagiotti, Cini Boeri, Laura Bonaparte, Nino Brandolini, Giuliana di Camerino, Thomas and Sandra Campaniello, Helietta Caracciolo, Viviana Carrozini, Letitia Cerio, the staff at Christie's, Anna Maria Cicogna, Gianni Cigna, Madame Marie-Louise de Clermont-Tonnere, Anne Marie Cloutier, Marilyn Cooperman, Rudi Crespi, Linda Dannenberg, Jean Louis and Lynn Sutherland David, Fiammetta Fadda, Alda Fendi, Gianfranco Ferrè, Jack Flanagan, Maud Frizon, Anastasia de la Fuente, Sophie Galeras, Nives Gambarana, Carol and Ira Garey, Louis Gartner, Vittorio Gregotti, the staff at the Guggenheim, Enrico Job, Margaret Kennedy, Chicca Lalatta, Hedi Giusti Lanham, Charla Lawhon, Douglas Lewis, Vittorio Licari, Graziella Lonardi, Pablo Manzoni, Gabriella Mariotti, Aris and Glenn Marziali, the Metropolitan Museum of Art, Francesco Miani, Betti Missoni, Tai and Rosita Missoni, Dan Moriarity, Bruno Munari, Ron Nicolaysen, Roberto Orlandi, Jean Paul, Lili Peinetti, Mirella Peteni, Robert Phelan, Sr., Denis Piel, Carol Manchester Pillay, Piero Pinto, Pierfrancesco Prosperi, Maria Grazia Raimondi, Priscilla Rattazzi, Lisa Ricasoli, James Roderick, Richard and Julie Rush, Rand Sagers, Giorgio Saporiti, Piero Sartogo, Franco Sartori, William Kent Schoenfish, Livio de Simone, Sloane Simpson, the staff at Sotheby's, Ettore Sottsass, Robert Talignani, Zipora Tehilim, Adam Tihany, Bernard and Beatrice Traissac, Isa Vercelloni, Gianni Versace, Graziella Vigo, Nanda Vigo, Egon Von Furstenberg, Marco Zanuso, and Anna Zegna.

Our appreciation to Paola Acquati, Annalisa Ferrari, Riccardo and Stefania Gambarana, Carla Lesh, Barbara Lessona, Marian Nammack, and Scott Osmond for their help.

Catherine Sabino, New York
Angelo Tondini, Milan
January 1985

CONTENTS

WHAT IS ITALIAN STYLE?

"Italian style demonstrates an attention to a visual image that's almost impossible to find elsewhere. It's a result of an extraordinary creativity, fantasy, sense of color and proportion, love of elegance, and quality of life. It also is due to the finely balanced equilibrium between industry and craftsmanship—an industrial product produced in Italy can have the quality and prestige of one produced by an artisan's hands. This applies particularly to the production of furniture. But in today's interiors one also sees the role of the artisan in the details and the finish. Italian style strikes a personal equilibrium between old and new things, between custom-designed objects and those industrially produced, always trying, depending on the context, a new and diverse mode of appearing."

Isa Vercelloni, editor-in-chief, *Casa Vogue*

"Italian style is very complex and difficult to pigeonhole from an aesthetic point of view. I would put the word 'style' in quotations because it suggests a codification that's already distinct. I attribute the success of Italian 'style' regarding interior decoration to the following factors: 1. Most Italian interior designers are architects; as a result they have a global cultural background and a unique sense of the context of space in which they must operate. Only in Italy do we have this combination of interior designer/architect. In other countries they are generally quite separate occupations. 2. Regarding furniture production: There is an economic structure and tradition that still permits an artisan culture and is very important because Italians demand the highest quality product. 3. Italian taste is among the most refined in the world, derived from a tradition cultivated over the centuries."

Gae Aulenti, architect and industrial designer

"The success of Italian style is due in large part to its architects and artisans. Italians have always been fortunate to have the marvelous tradition of the craftsman who revives and keeps alive the techniques used in the past. Besides, Italian designers are flexible, adapt marvelously to the demands of the marketplace, and are open to input from other fields. Italian fashion and design were born independently of one another, but now the cross influences are frequent. And what they both have in common is a research and care for materials."

Piero Pinto, interior designer

"Italian style today in each of its manifestations from Armani to Memphis is the fruit of a general cultural state of faith in better communication in the self-definition of each of us, in the personal choice of a life-style and not in the imposition from above of rules and modes of behavior. Italian design today is becoming more democratic because its designers seek constantly to create more comprehensible images for even the political strata which would be least prepared to absorb them."

Ettore Sottsass, architect and industrial designer

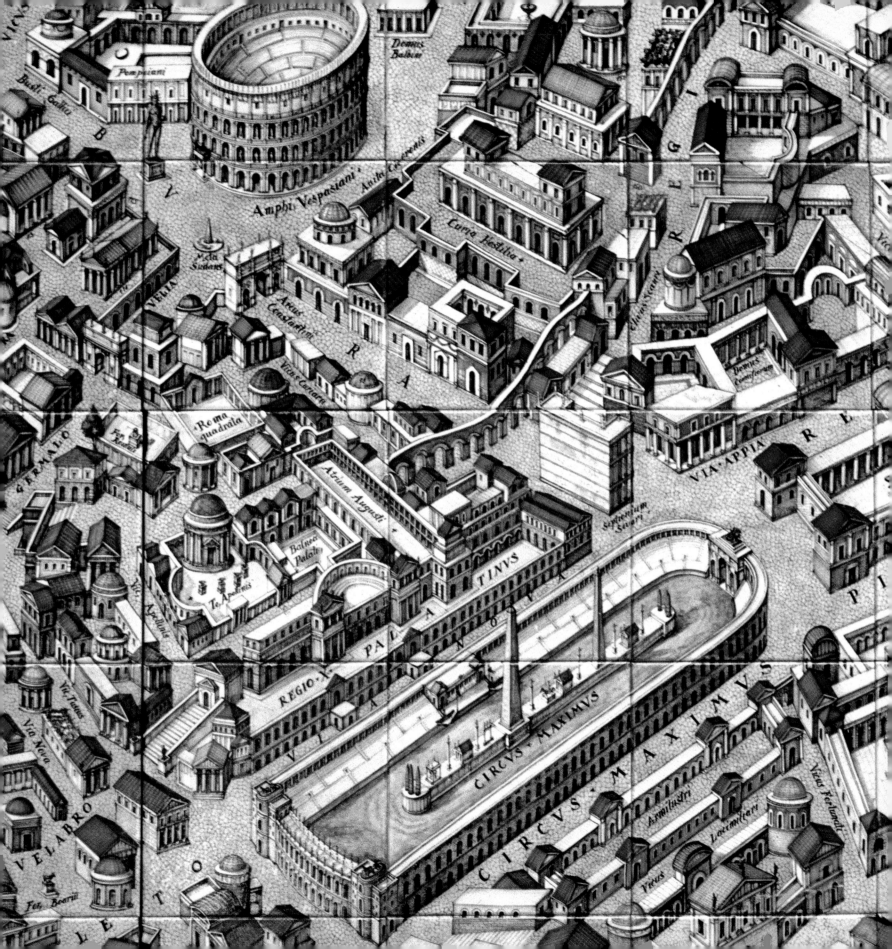

INTRODUCTION

There is no one typical Italian interior, just as there really is no one representative Italian city or one characteristic Italian dish. Venice is as Italian as Taormina, risotto as Italian as insalata Caprese, and a restored medieval castle in the Roman countryside as appropriately Italian as a small apartment filled with the visionary "Infinite" furniture from Studio Alchimia. There isn't a singular Italian look quickly reproducible by the purchase of yards of fabric or antiques of a certain period.

Italian interior design style, whether it be traditional, modern, or avant-garde, reflects the Italian passion for quality, an eye for contrast, a seemingly intuitive ability to mix periods in an imaginative yet understated way. It also reflects a characteristic individuality in approach, even when the budgets are large and the most skilled interior designers are enlisted. A room is never just decorated: Clients and designers work closely together in planning, sometimes with a spirited sense of competitiveness to see who might find the rare antique or most suitable period rug. Most interior designers in Italy are architects, which as Marco Zanuso, the prominent architect and industrial designer, says, allows for "a precisely balanced relationship between furniture, decorative objects, and household equipment and a harmonious blending of color, materials, and dimensions."

The rooms in many Italian homes, particularly those found in *palazzi* (the Italian word for palace, but also the term used for grand or city structures), *villas* (country houses), and *castelli* (castles), have museumlike proportions; they were built with high ceilings, thick walls, and marble floors to contend with long, hot Mediterranean summers and their owner's notion of grandeur. The abundance of these enormous high-ceilinged spaces has prevented Italian designers from developing a cozy style that can be found in certain English and French homes. But their size, along with splendidly embellished walls, lined with marble or silk, elaborately painted with frescoes, enriched with bas-reliefs, statue-filled niches, and flooring of terrazzo or intricate marble mosaic, has also precluded a design approach that is overfurnished and overaccessorized.

The largest room in most Italian homes is the *soggiorno*—the living or drawing room. In some of Italy's older and grander residences, it was typical to find a *soggiorno* and several smaller, more intimate *salotti,* or sitting rooms. The concept of multiple living rooms extends to the present with both winter and summer *soggiorni* re-created in many of the older structures and sometimes created in modern villas, too. These *soggiorni,* as in previous centuries, are used seasonally, distinguished by furnishings, fabric coverings, and color schemes that suggest a suitable warmth or an airy freshness. In modern apartments, where a comparable luxury of space may be lacking, an expansive *soggiorno* is sometimes created out of several smaller rooms, the new area organized into various conversation, dining, and entertainment zones, fully equipped with the latest television, video, and musical equipment. Another more informal room used for home entertaining and in recent years for exercising—Italians coming late but no less enthusiastically than Americans to the desire for fitness—is the *sala relax,* the Italian equivalent of a recreation room.

The *sala da pranzo,* or dining room, is one of the more frequently used rooms in the Italian house, with many families, even in Italy's most modern urban centers, assembling in it twice a day, at one, the *ora di pranzo,* the time of the main meal, and at eight or later for a light *cena,* or snack. The expansive and hospitable Italian personality finds frequent expression in home entertaining, which while always a mainstay of Italian social life has become even more popular in recent years. An invitation to a private home is still viewed as the most gracious extension of Italian hospitality.

The *cucina,* or kitchen, once strictly a service room, has in postwar Italian society been given new attention and importance. In this extremely food-conscious nation encompassing many fine regional cuisines, cooking is a favored pastime that is no longer the exclusive domain of the *signora* or the *nonna* (grandmother), who never consulted a cookbook in her life. Today, wives of Milanese industrialists frequently spend as much time in them as their cooks, and single men and women pride themselves in preparing family specialties and do so even in the tiniest of rooms. In the country the kitchen continues as a tribal gathering spot, decorated with colorful tiles, ceramics, earthenware, and rustic furniture.

In most *villas* and *palazzi,* public and private quarters have been organized since the days of the Renaissance on separate levels, with the *soggiorno, salotti, sala da pranzo,* library, and perhaps a music and reading room occupying the *piano nobile,* or first floor, and bedrooms, baths, and private studies on the second and third floors. The rooms on each level open to a long spacious corridor, which is sometimes furnished with consoles, mirrors, small tables, and divans. In modern villas and apartments with a single floor, public and private areas can be separated by corridors, partial walls, graduated levels, or even more simply by the color of the walls. *Camere da letto,* or bedrooms, can be clean-lined and modern or elaborately romantic, yet many are minimally furnished even if the pieces are antiques. Due to the contrast between the large rooms and their limited furnishings, many Italian bedrooms appear almost stark to the American eye.

Il bagno, or the bathroom, may have the same lavish wall treatments and flooring found in the other rooms of an Italian home, the extravagant bath a tradition since Roman times. Beautifully colored marble tubs, tiles, paintings, grisailles, classic statues, Art Deco figurines, and antique dressing tables often embellish a bathroom's interior, but more contemporary versions are precisely planned spaces that make the most of every square centimeter with the latest custom-made fixtures.

Many rooms in the Italian home open to a terrazzo, or a small balcony, or face whenever possible on to splendidly landscaped gardens. Surrounded by some of the most beautiful countryside in the world, Italians are also fond of bringing nature indoors, whether it be in the form of interior or winter gardens, sometimes so small that they fit into the confines of a glass-topped cupola, or by simply using the same flooring indoors as found in an exterior courtyard or on a set of outdoor stairs.

The Italian love for nature extends to a passion for vacation homes. With a profusion of glorious mountains, glittering lakes, a seductive seaside, and an abundance of exotic islands, most Italians view *le vacanze,* or vacation, and the getaway weekend with a sense of entitlement. Vacation homes can be modest or grand, a small seaside apartment or a sizable lakeside villa, decorated simply with furniture upholstered in white cotton or canvas or, depending on the style of the villa, with magnificent antiques or the best examples of modern Italian design.

Traditional rooms are rarely furnished with antiques from a single period: A "total" look is as alien in Italy as ham-and-eggs for breakfast. Renaissance pieces may be mixed with antiques from the Orient and the furnishings in one room can vary in age by as many as 2,000 years—Italians having not one but several glorious pasts: classical, Renaissance, and baroque. Foreign influences abound, not surprisingly in a country that before unification in 1870 fell prey to numerous invasions by the French, Spanish, and Austrians. Empire was particularly popular during the early 1800s due to the presence of Napoleon and his relatives in Italy: His sister Pauline married into the Roman Borghese family and a stepson was viceroy of Naples.

Bored by the *fin de siècle* jumble of revivals, early 20th-century Italians embraced *lo stile floreale,* the Italian term for Art Nouveau; it was the hit of the Turin Exposition in 1904. Enresto Basile and Eugenio Quarti created furniture designs with appropriate *floreale* ornamentation, but the taste for *floreale,* despite its initial popularity, was brief, with some of its most enthusiastic admirers—in Italy, anyway—appearing in later decades.

Futurism, an iconoclastic reaction against the *floreale* style, as well as most vestiges of the past, was next to rise to artistic and architectural eminence. While some futurists such as Giacomo Balla designed chimerical, avant-garde furniture, the production of these pieces was minimal and they seem to belong more to the annals of futuristic art than to the antecedents of modern Italian furniture design.

Between the wars Art Deco was extremely popular, and a boon to Italian cabinetmakers and furniture manufacturers who, in response to Mussolini's ban on foreign importations, produced their own versions of the jazzy, striking French and English pieces. In the late 1920s and early 1930s, advocates of Italian Rationalism, particularly the Gruppo Seven team formed in Milan, decried the tenets of Futurism, while trying their own hand at styling interiors, most notably at the Fifth Triennial Exhibition in 1933. Even if it was the spirit of the German Werkbund that inspired them, the creations of members Gabriele Mucchi and Franco Albini, as well as Enrico Peressutti, Ernesto Rogers, and Giò Ponti, lay the groundwork for the extraordinary energy and modernism of Italian design after the Second World War.

Rationalist in spirit, postwar design sought to bring Italian society into the present and wherever possible to aid in the country's economic and cultural restructuring. Signaling to the world Italian inventiveness and quality, it was quick to gain an international reputation—Nizzoli's work for Olivetti; the Necchi sewing machine; Pininfarina's automotive design, particularly the archetypal Cisitalia and his prototypes for Lancia and Ferrari; the scooters, Piaggio's "Vespa" and Innocenti's "Lambretta"; Nuccio Bertone's designs for Alfa Romeo. Architect/designers sought to develop furniture that had a popular appeal, multiple uses, and new materials—for home furnishings at least. Chairs, sofas, beds, and kitchen units were manufactured from steel, foam rubber, sheet metal, aluminum, reinforced polyester, materials associated more traditionally with an automobile assembly line. And it was the Italians' successful and innovative work with plastics that revolutionized the furniture industry and brought about the greatest transformation in chair design since Thonet. (The first chair made entirely of plastic was designed by Marco Zanuso and Richard Sapper for Kartell in 1963.)

What made modern Italian design unique? Only in Italy was the working relationship between designer and industrial technician as symbiotic, with the designer an integral part of all phases of the actual production process. Other factors included the importance given to aesthetic considerations in the overall design process, an accommodation to economic constraints that often resulted in a simpler, more coherent product, and an uncanny perception of design and style that reached beyond the whims of momentary fashion. Behind it all, the Italian architects, whose training and cultural backgrounds were as varied as the Italian landscape, whose visions were limitless, could feel equally adept at designing a stage set or a coffeepot. They carried on with their eclectic design activities in many fields, appropriate heirs to the design legacy of their Renaissance and baroque ancestors.

Clever design, witty design, experimental design, as well as remarkably functional design, geared to be available and affordable to a wide public, originated from architects' and designers' drawing boards with astonishing frequency. Marco Zanuso, Mario Bellini, Vico Magistretti, Gae Aulenti, Ettore Sottsass among others, with their adventurous talent and prodigious productivity, transformed the world of design; their accomplishments were affirmed repeatedly in the international marketplace, at the annual Milan Furniture Fair, which began in 1960, as well as in the quieter realms of museums both here and abroad, that collected and displayed their work. In 1972, the Museum of Modern Art's exhibit *Italy: The New Domestic Landscape* celebrated the genius of post–World War II architects and designers while exploring the conformist, reformist, and radical components of their work.

Modern design underwent a period of reevaluation in the mid-1970s with some of its most stalwart proponents now nodding to the past, sometimes in playful, irreverent contexts, sometimes by incorporating features of earlier avant-garde movements, most notably at Studio Alchimia with its distinctly bizarre offerings of neomodern furniture. It paved the way for the so-called New International Style that Memphis came to symbolize in the early 1980s. Memphis, like Alchimia, an experimental furniture design collective, includes such famed international designers and architects as Michael Graves, Arata Isozaki, and Javier Mariscal under the leadership of Ettore Sottsass. It has called itself "a bubbling cauldron of mutations": Furniture is developed to broaden the concept and context of design while suggesting a new catalogue of signs and imagery. Form doesn't necessarily have to follow function, and historical allusions are often interpreted in witty, exaggerated, and highly original ways.

Media acceptance for these design collectives was initially stronger than that of the consumer, but the advocates and devotees, particularly of Memphis, are growing, their champions secure. Alessandro Mendini, the editorial director of the architectural magazine *Domus*, says, "By now it's only a question of time—the image of Italian furniture will change beyond recognition."

Perhaps. While there are few apartments or villas completely furnished with avant-garde furniture, many Italians applaud the bold steps taken by Studio Alchimia or Memphis in challenging the notions of furniture design. The iconography of Memphis has already spread to the more conservative reaches of the Italian furniture industry and other areas as well, its pieces even being sold at retail in the American Midwest.

Italians have lived with exceptional design for over two thousand years and instinctively know a good thing when they see it. Flash-in-the-pan trends find a harder time taking root in Italy than in other countries, history seeming to have created less fertile soil for the substanceless and trendy. Whether furnishing a primary residence or vacation home in a traditional style, with modern pieces or in rarer instances with the iconoclastic offerings of the avant-garde, Italians have perhaps the most remarkable inventory of design from which to draw. In recent years many have sought to make their interior environments warmer, more personal, often exchanging the sleek design of the 1960s and early 1970s for a mix of antiques and contemporary pieces, sometimes opting for the work of Thonet, Hoffmann, Ruhlmann, and other masters of "early modern" design as well as for pieces from the *floreale* and Art Deco periods.

In spite of the strides made by the most avant-garde of the Italian designers' collectives, the lure of the past will always remain powerful in Italy. Says Achille Castiglioni, "All our culture is made of memory." At the close of the 20th century, Italian interior style can be characterized by a melting pot of design periods and outlooks, not dissimilar in variety to the eclecticism that marked the end of the 1800s.

We have organized *Italian Style* into three sections, which we feel best reflect the expressions of Italian interior design style today: traditional, modern, and avant-garde. Our cutoff point for the traditional section was the end of the 19th century; the apartments decorated in the style of the early 20th century are placed in the modern section, for it was the Art Nouveau movement that helped make Italy aware of the contemporary trends beyond her borders and led her into the modern design era. By including the very old and the very new, we hope to show the richness of the style, with all its enigmatic contrasts, its centuries-spanning scope, and flexible inventiveness. There is a harmony and continuity within Italian style, a serenity in the midst of change that comes from the Italians themselves, an endlessly fascinating people whose most instinctive vocation and most memorable export is their taste for the beautiful.

LA TRADIZ

A traditional Italian residence can range from a restored medieval castle in the Roman countryside to a compact Milanese apartment furnished casually with family antiques. Italians, taking a cue from their surroundings—the layers of history that blend remnants of classical, medieval, Renaissance, and baroque epochs—are adept at mixing a wide range of antiques. And while the past is cherished, it is never allowed to be intimidating; centuries-old pieces are lived with in ways that suit contemporary personal needs. Houses with carefully restored Renaissance frescoes, with intricate moldings, and grand and imposing sweeps of space nonetheless convey a sense of intimacy, a human spirit that is a hallmark of the Italian character. The traditional style, ever popular in Italy, is today in even greater favor, frequently replacing the sleekly modern look of the last decades.

The Castello di Marco Simone has 59 rooms and a central tower that is nearly 1,000 years old, below. A 14th-century weather vane from Umbria, a region in central Italy, over-looks the walls of the courtyard, right, which links the Biagiotti studio and showrooms with the castle. Roman columns uncovered in the restoration can be viewed near one wall.

biagiotti

RESTORING A ROMAN COUNTRY CASTLE

The newspaper ad stated simply, "Castle for Sale." Yet it was intriguing enough for Laura Biagiotti, the fashion designer and former archaeology student, to travel to the Roman countryside for a firsthand look. What she found was the Castello di Marco Simone in a sorry state of decay; regardless, it was *un colpo di fulmine,* "love at first sight," and the beginning of a mammoth four-year restoration she undertook with Gianni Cigna, president of Biagiotti Exports.

"At the outset, it was just an intriguing big ruin," says Piero Pinto, the Milanese architect who oversaw the project. The property was the former site of a Roman villa. Built from the 11th through the 15th centuries, the existing castle had been home to many noble families, among them the Borghese, but had fallen into neglect in the 17th century.

Pinto's goal was to make the 59-room castle and its adjoining buildings livable, while preserving their historical significance. The most pressing structural problem was to join the first and second floors, which until then had been linked only by an outside stairway. Based on clues from excavations, Pinto re-created an interior passageway, and thereby avoided restructuring a sizable part of the castle. Priceless frescoes, stucco, and 19th-century neo-Gothic paintings were discovered and restored.

Adamant about keeping interior furnishings "unpretentious, the way an Italian country home should be," Pinto combined styles with nonchalance. Regional brick and ceramic tiles were used for flooring, and the Roman stucco, called *pozzolana,* for the walls.

With the major renovations completed, Laura Biagiotti's castle has become a unique living place—and, as architectural historian Jean Coste has said, one that represents "the most spectacular restorative work of a historical site in the Roman countryside."

The small foyer leads directly to the summer drawing room. Herringbone-patterned pavement, made from recycled brick, also found in the interior courtyard, unites the indoors and outdoors. The black 19th-century divan is trimmed in ebony.

The bas-relief marble medallion, left, crafted in Italy during the 18th century, is part of a pair that flanks the walls of the entrance foyer. The pastel glow of a Roman sunset colors the pool area, below. The geometric pool has a shape identical to that of the perimeter of the castle wall. The bottom of the pool is lined with pebbles taken from the Tiber River.

White and black Ceramica Musa tiles in a pattern inspired by the 19th century line the sun-filled country kitchen. The marble-topped antique table, called a *fratina,* provides a spacious area for food preparation. The stone imposts of the ceiling arches were left unpainted.

The summer drawing room on the first floor is described by Laura Biagiotti as the "freshest room in the castle." Handmade tiles varying in degrees of translucent whiteness are arranged in geometric patterns. The vaulted ceiling is part of the castle's original structure and dates from the 14th century. Now serving as a bar, the 17th-century side cabinets were once owned by a Piedmontese pharmacist.

Used for entertaining during the winter months, the second-floor drawing room is rich and inviting with furniture upholstered in luxurious fabrics. The Roman statue and the *armadio,* or cupboard, as well as the lavish gold-embroidered Genovese cloth covering a table topped with small Etruscan vases and busts, are from the 18th century. The remnants of pitchers, right, are also Etruscan.

A view of the opposite end of the drawing room shows the 16th-century frescoes that grace its walls, a low round contemporary marble table displaying an assortment of Etruscan objects, and an antique Chinese rug.

The *zona degli affreschi,* or fresco area, on the second floor of the castle consists of three rooms and a loggia. Primarily from the 15th and 16th centuries with some dating from Roman times and transported to the castle from other villas, the frescoes were discovered under nine coats of paint by Laura Biagiotti. It took five artists from the *Sovrintendenza alle Belle Arti,* a Roman preservation committee, one and a half years to restore them. The frescoes in the loggia, left, believed to have been inspired by those of Raffaello in the Vatican, depict a variety of divinities and naturalistic themes. Subjects are predominantly astrological and mythological in the restored fresco rooms. An angel head is portrayed, above, an early 16th-century allegorical figure of summer is represented, far right, and a family crest emblazoned, right, over the original 16th-century travertine marble fireplace. The fresco rooms have no furniture and remain rooms of passage.

In Biagiotti's bedroom, the white-beamed ceiling, embellished with gold moons and stars, adds a touch of fantasy. The window in the bedroom's breakfast nook, right, overlooks the Roman countryside. The coffee service is by Ginori.

To make the enormous bedroom seem personal and romantic, walls, windows, and bed were draped with fine gold-threaded white Italian silk. The *baldacchino* bed with its sweeping veiled canopy is of cherrywood and bronze and was crafted in France in 1830.

In another part of the bedroom, a 19th-century sofa recovered in white fabric was placed in front of frescoes that were removed from the castle's chapel. White silk curtains filter the soft Roman light.

Biagiotti is an impassioned collector. The fans, along with the ivory pieces, span a variety of epochs and countries of origin. The Tuscan bureau, below and right, is from the 18th century and is placed in a corridor near the bedroom.

The brick and marble structure, right, formerly a chapel, is located in the heart of Venice on property that has been a church site since the 10th century. Converted into a private house in the 1930s, the building was discovered by Piero Pinto during a work assignment in the region. Because he found the main interior space too high, Pinto added a large gridiron floor that divided it into two levels, far right.

pinto

VENETIAN FANTASY IN A FORMER CHAPEL

"I found it by chance," says Piero Pinto, of the compact brick and marble *palazzo*, a former chapel, that has become his fourth home. "At the beginning," recalls Pinto, "it was only a dark, narrow, high space without any sense of its past. Previous owners felt there should be no evidence that it was a church. But I was determined to start with the original structure." As a result his restoration uncovered antique brick walls and floors composed of a variety of marble inlays.

Located in a *piazzetta* near the Ponte dell'Accademia off the Grand Canal, the church was at its inception a typical three-naved Byzantine basilica and was transformed numerous times over the centuries. Now only the chapel remains, as a result of the last reconstruction, in 1865. Although an owner of residences in Milán, Varese, and Monte Marcello, a small village near the Italian Riviera, Pinto has a particular affinity for his home in Venice, which he describes as "a special sort of dream; it corresponds to my state of mind." The son of one of Egypt's most successful cotton traders and a native of Alexandria, he claims the chapel is "a blending of East and West." Furnishings include Italian antiques from the 18th and 19th centuries often covered in cashmeres and Fortuny-inspired velvets, as well as Italian contemporary pieces. Eastern accents appear throughout in Persian rugs, Egyptian statues, Chinese boxes, and Turkish paperweights.

The living area is divided horizontally by a metal-grid floor, which supports a casual conversation zone above the more formal sitting room. Light filters through the grid, producing a latticework effect, illuminating the delicately colored marbles—the Verona red, the Botticino beige, and ivory-white Pietra d'Istria lining the walls and floors of the ground level. The iron flooring was designed with the assistance of Francesco Zanon of Venice, according to the particular dimensions of the chapel space.

A tranquil *piazzetta* near the Grand Canal can be glimpsed through an iron grillwork window in the first-floor living area. The motif is typically Venetian, designed to recall the waves of the sea.

When viewed from the ground floor, the gridiron landing that divides the main chapel space into two levels forms an interesting abstract pattern with the chapel's vaulted ceiling, which was painted white during the restoration.

Columns made of Verona marble separate a small cozy sitting area from the living room. The openwork window in the background is based on the Arab *moucharaby,* devised so that one could view the outside world without being seen.

A Piedmontese military bed from the 18th century, covered with a French tapestry from the same period, lies at the base of a marbleized wood table in the living room, left. Three colors of marble, Pietra d'Istria ivory, Botticino beige, and Verona red, cover the walls and floor. Greeting all visitors is a door knocker made from a 19th-century bronze lion's head, below.

The framed wire sculpture by the Italian abstract artist Fausto Melotti, located above the sofa in the living area, below, is frequently moved to different locations in the house. The sofa is upholstered in a swirling print fabric by Naj-Oleari, which picks up the pattern of the marble walls and floors. Light filtering through the gridiron floor creates geometric designs on the walls, right.

Traces of the East are present in a small first-floor bedroom, above, where the painted terracotta busts are Egyptian and the rug is Persian. French and English 19th-century mirrors distort images in an almost magical way. Piero Pinto's fondness for mixing different periods of furniture is evident in another first-floor bedroom, right. A Regency chair sits at the entrance, the cherrywood and ebony *cassettone* is a neo-Gothic piece from Lucca, and the chair beneath the window is in the French Restoration style.

The beautifully restored brick walls are part of the original structure and most visible on the second level of the former chapel, below. In the informally furnished sitting room the central table and shelving are dotted with Pinto's extensive collection of Turkish and Venetian paperweights and vases. Some of the most colorful glass pieces are from Venice and surround the French 19th-century painting, left.

The Tizio lamp by Artemide, which lights a delicate arrangement of Murano glass, left, and the vase designed by Ettore Sottsass, above, are modern accents in the sitting room.

A statue of Catherine Cornaro, the grandmother of the villa's original owner and once the queen of Cyprus, is located in a niche in the Villa Cornaro's central hall, right. The trompe l'oeil fresco painted to seem like a bas-relief, far right, is framed by one that was carved by Cabianca, an artisan well known in the Veneto during the 18th century. The draped cloth molding is accented with *putti*, or cherubs, a motif that appears frequently in Italian painting and sculpture from the Renaissance to the 18th-century Rococo period.

rush

When the Venetian Senate passed a bill in the 16th century encouraging land recla mation in the swampy countryside neighboring Venice, vil las designed by Andrea Palladio and his students and imitators in creasingly graced the Veneto land- scape. Beginning in 1530 and con tinuing for over 60 years, many of Venice's wealthiest citizens under took the construction of country houses. Space was abundant as it had never been in Venice and the new landowners sought to build homes with expansive grandeur, but with more reason ably priced materials than the marbles that filled their consid erably smaller *palazzi* in town. Palladio, who embraced the ancient Romans' love of symmetry, harmony, and clean-lined splendor, accommodated his clients' wishes for reasonable economy by building the villas in rough brickwork, finished by a stucco coating. Columns were similarly constructed, with intricate and more costly detailing reserved for column bases and capitals.

The Rush home, known as the Villa Cornaro after its original owners, is one of many villas Palladio designed for the Venetian countryside during this period. His last remaining house with a double-level projecting portico, it has had notable imitations: Thomas Jefferson showed a similar portico in his original sketches for Monticello as well as in his anonymously submitted competition designs for the U.S. Capitol.

The Villa Cornaro was restored over a 14-year period by its owners, Richard and Julie Rush of Connecticut, who have worked closely on the project with the government preservation agency, Ente Per Le Ville Venete. Over 18 rooms fill two identically designed floors. The central hall of the *piano nobile,* the main floor, has been kept spare and overlooks the graceful harmony of the lower-level portico and gardens.

The Villa Cornaro is in the village of Piombino Dese, about 20 miles from Venice. The house is open to the public on Saturdays during the eight weeks each year the Rushes are in residence or by appointment with the custodian.

As the Ente Per Le Ville Venete, the area's preservation agency, does not allow standard paint to be used on the exteriors of Palladian villas, a special formula of pulverized marble, brick powder, and stucco was created to restore the facade.

The north facade of the Villa Cornaro, with its widely imitated double-level projecting portico, has Ionic and Corinthian columns. The enormous stone sphere was probably added as an ornamental element during the 18th century when the villa's gardens were redesigned.

Renaissance ceilings were often elaborately decorated. An 18th-century Venetian chandelier hangs from the ceiling of the main floor central hall, which was hand-painted under Palladio's supervision during the 16th century.

The *salone grande*, right, contains frescoes by Mattia Bortoloni, an 18th-century painter. Furnishings have been kept minimal so as not to detract from the elaborate frescoes, wall moldings, and bas-reliefs.

Manicured boxwood hedges grace the entrance to the Villa Emo, below. The villa, completed in 1588, stands behind a *cancello,* or gate, right, modeled after one designed by Palladio in Vincenza.

FARMHOUSE RETURNED TO CLASSIC SPLENDOR

It was a monumental task of restoration. The villa, used for centuries as a granary, still accommodated a ton of corn. But Countess Giuseppina Emo (*nata* Pignatelli) wanted to finish the refurbishing as quickly as possible and did so in little over fifteen months. The house has since become the year-round residence of the Emos and a frequent retreat for their daughter, Marina, and their grandchildren.

Completed in 1588, eight years after Palladio's death, the villa was most likely designed by Vincenzo Scamozzi, one of the most talented and prominent of Palladio's followers. A Scamozzi villa demonstrated the same classic splendor as those of his illustrious master, if on a slightly smaller scale. For example, Palladio's Malcontenta near Venice probably served as inspiration for Villa Emo, although Scamozzi chose to construct a four-columned portico rather than replicate the larger building's six-columned entrance.

Spacious public rooms and more compact private chambers fill the three-story villa, which is rich in frescoes by Bernardino India and Giovan Battista del Moro, artists who worked in the Veneto during the late Renaissance. While restoring the villa, the countess uncovered some of India's frescoes decorating the main drawing room's vaulted ceiling and had the wall frescoes by Del Moro, depicting the four seasons, framed with trompe l'oeil architectural elements.

A formal stretch of gardens leads to a maze of tree-lined walking paths. Soft pink gravel called *trachite di Verona* surrounds a swirl of manicured boxwood trained to form a monogram of the owner's initials. Carefully tended rose beds fill other parts of the garden that were once produce fields. The roses are passionately cultivated by the countess, who arranges them in bouquets that adorn every room of the house.

Four 18th-century busts rest on a table crafted in the 1500s, which stands in front of one of the Del Moro frescoes in the *salone grande,* or main drawing room, left. The shimmery terrazzo flooring, made of crushed marble and terra-cotta, was frequently found in the grand houses of the 16th century.

The main drawing room of the Villa Emo, below, is sectioned into several conversation zones with an assortment of Venetian antiques. The frescoes on the barrel-vaulted ceiling were completed near the end of the 16th century by Bernardino India. One of Countess Emo's floral arrangements, below right, rests on a table with antique Turkish fabric and glass.

Local craftsmen restored the delicate frescoes by Bernardino India, above. The detail of the ceiling fresco shows a graceful arabesque. During the 15th and 16th centuries, the *cassone,* right, was an important piece of furniture in the Italian home. Embellished by carved-relief patterns, it was used for storage, as a dowry chest, or as a trunk when traveling. The *cassone* in the *salone grande* dates from Renaissance times.

Trompe l'oeil architectural elements frame each of the Del Moro frescoes. An 18th-century Venetian settee, upholstered in silk, right, is positioned in the main drawing room beneath a depiction of *Spring*.

The exquisite black *monetario*, which once held coin collections, is located in a ground-floor drawing room. The *monetario* was originally a piece of furniture used for transporting money or valuables and was most commonly found in Naples or Sicily.

The glass panels of the *monetario* were individually hand-painted in oil when the piece was crafted in Naples during the 17th century.

An 18th-century Venetian landscape, above, hangs over the tiled fireplace of the *salotto verde,* or green room. The *salotto,* right, is a small, intimate drawing room on the main floor. Chairs and sofas are Venetian antiques, upholstered in green silk.

Countess Emo's collection of fans, glass, porcelain, and Neapolitan faïence fills an 18th-century *angoliera,* or corner cabinet, left. The giltwood marble-topped console, above, is typical of 18th-century Venice's highly decorative style. The pendulum clock is Austrian, the fresco by Del Moro.

The copper cookware and ceramic tureens, right and below right, dating from the 19th century, were collected from the nearby region of Monselice by the Emos' daughter, Marina.

The beautifully refurbished country-style kitchen is used for informal meals and is located in the six-room cottage, La Barchessa, adjacent to the Villa Emo. The cottage, a former 16th-century stable, was restored by Marina for her own use. The long wooden table is from the Renaissance, the sink from the 18th century.

Palladio and his followers designed their villas so that the rooms looked out on expansive, beautifully proportioned gardens. The view of the well and the gardens of the villa, left, is from a first-floor window.

The large canvas market umbrella shades a stone dining table in one section of the garden, below. The countess's flowering bushes grow abundantly inside and around the villa walls.

Italian gardens have been elaborate since the days of Pompei, and some of the Renaissance's greatest architects, Palladio and Scamozzi among them, turned their hands to landscape design. Statue-lined walkways, spurting fountains, allegorical statues, manicured boxwood, and swimming pools were all elements of the *giardino all' italiana*. This *peschiera,* or fishpond, was probably designed by Scamozzi.

A classical statue sits a lonely guard at the end of the tree-lined corridor on the villa's grounds.

The entrance *salotto*, below, serves as a reading room and small reception area. The terracotta lacquered busts are by the Giustiniani, a well-known family of ceramicists who worked during the 19th century in Italy. Pillows, right, are covered in needlework from the 19th century. Cesare Rovatti, the interior architect of the villa, designed the small sofa.

fendi/caruso

Despite its state of disrepair, the Villa Cidonio had a special spirit and a promising potential that attracted Alda Fendi Caruso. Purchased in 1975, the house, located in a residential district in Rome, was restored at a leisurely and careful pace. "I didn't want to rush into deciding how the interior should look," says Caruso. "The villa had a strangely beautiful appeal in its emptiness. And I had to make up my mind as to which approach to take—furnishing the house completely or keeping it spare." On weekends she would go there, wander through the rooms, taking in its style. Certain existing elements— the portals, columns, and marble doors—and her own treasured collection of antiques convinced Caruso to restore the villa to its elaborate 19th-century style. Cesare Rovatti, a former design assistant to filmmaker Luchino Visconti, was chosen for the project.

Rovatti left the layout of the rooms untouched. The main floor flows smoothly from the entrance *salotto* through the *salone grande* to the music room and dining room. Upstairs a linear arrangement of bedrooms, baths, and study flanks a spacious hall. The furniture is an elaborate mix of Italian and French antiques, the latter often Empire. Among the most prized are four *sgabelli,* or stools, crafted by Pelagio Pelagi for the private apartments of the royal Savoia family.

The villa, with its harmony of windows and doors framed with shutters, overlooks 25 acres of property, which are brilliantly painted red, amber, and gold with every Roman sunset. A formal garden, once the site of a collection of more than seven thousand rose-bushes, lies buried beneath terraces and shrubbery and will soon be restored.

Two Tuscan cherrywood divans from the 19th century flank a marble statue of a mythological god in the entrance corridor, above. Vases are copies of Etruscan models. All wall treatments in the villa were designed by Arnaldo Copelli, a noted Milanese artist, who, like Cesare Rovatti, was a former assistant to Luchino Visconti. Breccia polychrome marble frames the entrance door, right.

An ebony console with brass inlays is crafted in the Second Empire style. The statue, a replica of the *Discus Thrower,* is from the same period. Faux marbre hand-painted walls repeat the mosaic pattern of the marble floor.

A Napoleon III gilt-bronze chandelier adds a soft warm light to the 19th-century-style *salone grande,* left. The silk damask and velvet sofas were designed by Rovatti. Two are positioned under large oil-painted panels from the Second Empire period, above. A third sofa in the center of the room, right, is covered in tapestry.

Faux bamboo shelves store lotions, powders, and creams in a second-floor bathroom. The fresco in the niche was painted during the 17th century.

The rustic breakfast room, adjacent to the kitchen, was planned for informal meals. An 18th-century English oak cupboard displays a collection of Ginori plates that harmonize with the blue-and-white-patterned tablecloth. The bentwood chairs are by Thonet.

Printed cotton chintz, used for lining walls and for bed coverings, lends a casual tone to the second-floor master bedroom with its Neapolitan brass bed.

The Empire-styled desk and chair from the early 19th century is used by Signora Caruso to tend to personal correspondence. The carpet is Aubusson.

The villa, built in the 1940s, has been in the Barbi family for two generations. Enormous urns filled with flowers grace niches in the foyer, below. Although the surroundings are tranquil and appear quite countrified, right, the residential zone is near one of the busiest sections in Rome.

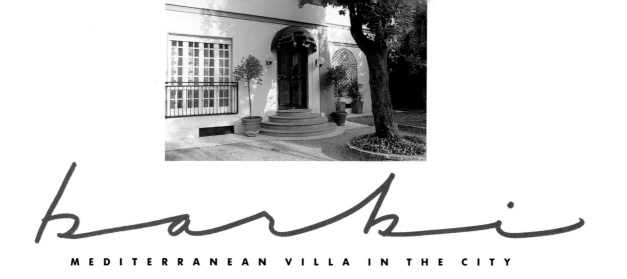

barbi

MEDITERRANEAN VILLA IN THE CITY

Once its surroundings were the tranquil Roman countryside, with the clamor of Rome just a rustle in the distance. But that was in the 1940s when the Villa Barbi was built. In recent decades the peaceful residential zone has become absorbed into the expanding city, yet the villa, sheltered by its private gardens, remains a treasured retreat for Tommaso Barbi, head of the Barbi International furniture company, and his family.

With the exception of a few exterior structural updates by architect Francesco Pensieri, the design of the two-story house has remained basically as it was when Barbi's father lived there. The layout of the interior is typical of many Mediterranean villas: corridors running the length of each floor, usually paved in marble to ensure coolness during the hot summer months; a linear succession of rooms that are parallel to the hallway, with public rooms for entertaining on the first level and bedrooms, studies, and baths on the second floor. Rooms traditionally open on to the corridor through a large intricately designed wood door, but doors here were eliminated between the living room and corridor and between the living and dining areas to keep the first floor free flowing and unrestricted. The wide entrances that remain are flanked by lacquered white half-columns.

The comfortably elegant decor of the first level suggests a subdued Mediterranean luxury. White and black marble tiles and the lacquered columns offset a mélange of antiques —Roman busts, Neapolitan bronzes, oversized urns, arrangements of obelisks, onyx and alabaster paperweights. Bedrooms reflect a highly personal style. One room is softly romantic, another masculine, with gray flannel walls, antique maps, and a collection of polo cups, and a third, which belongs to the Barbis' son, defined by a sporty plaid wall covering and antique prints.

A black-and-white-marble-tiled corridor leading to the living room ensures coolness during the hot Roman summer. Half-columns, painted in white lacquer, flank each first-level entranceway. Bronzes representing *Day* and *Night*, from the school of Jean de Bologne, top 19th-century pedestals.

The vivid colors of the abstract artist Giulio Turcato's painting, left, contrast with the black-and-white marble tiles. Obelisks in lapis, parchment, and tortoiseshell are arranged beneath it. The commode is French from the 19th century. Above the living room's white marble fireplace are de Chirico's *Polo Players*, sketched for Barbi when he was 18, and a Chalon bronze, below left. A collection of onyx, alabaster eggs, and paperweights rests on the floor.

The son's bedroom has an Empire-style bed, an old Vuitton chest, and an antique chaise. Prints depicting an assortment of turn-of-the-century carriages fill one wall.

In Signora Barbi's bedroom the *baldacchino* bed, above, designed by Barbi International, is draped in Italian silk, its soft ombré stripes harmonizing with the delicate floral fabric covering the walls. The *coiffeuse* is from the Charles X period, the drawing is by Salvador Dali. In an adjacent bathroom, right, a *floreale*, or Italian Art Nouveau, statue rests near a marble tub with Art Deco-style trim.

Signor Barbi's bedroom
includes a collection of antique
maps and the polo cups he's
won in various tournaments,
right. A beautifully preserved
Italian commode from the
1700s, below, displays silver
pieces from Bahia and ostrich
eggs in the living room.

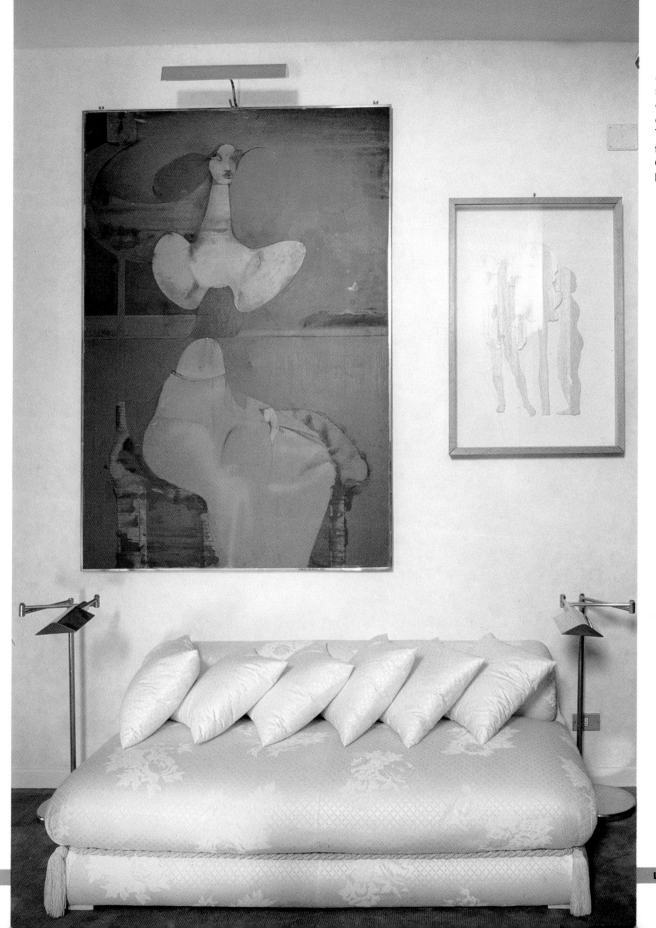

An informal sitting area outside the upstairs bedrooms has a silk-covered sofa and lamps designed by Barbi International. The painting is by Emile Aubri; to its right is a collage by Mario Ceroli, a noted contemporary Italian sculptor.

Built in the 18th century and restored in 1973, the farmhouse, below, was once the site of a foundation that raised funds for the Florentine foundling hospital, Ospedale degli Innocenti, designed by Brunelleschi. A stone medallion placed in one villa wall recalls that past, right.

ferragamo/ san giuliano

REBUILDING A FARMHOUSE NEAR FLORENCE

Italian architects who take on the task of restoring a farmhouse often have to contend with such agrarian holdovers as former animal stalls and granary storage areas—but such projects do provide the opportunity to create living quarters that are airy and spacious. This farmhouse, located 30 kilometers from Florence, dates from 1783 and was restored by architect Roberto Monsani as a weekend home for the Marchese and Marchesa di San Giuliano; she is Fiamma Ferragamo.

Its first floor was an animal stall from which Signor Monsani structured a large living area, dining room, library, and kitchen. Seven bedrooms and five baths fill the upper level, the farmhouse's original living quarters, once linked to the ground floor via an exterior staircase. The staircase was removed and replaced by one in white painted wood, which is now located in the center of the house.

Corridors with open-paneled ceilings and stairs constructed from simple slats of wood allow a radiant light to filter through both levels. White walls, large rooms, and furniture covered in casual printed fabric add to the sense of brightness. The antiques, generally from the Florentine countryside, are complemented by the rustic wood-beamed ceilings, stone hearths, brightly colored ceramic dishes—and from second-level windows, by the panoramic view of the vineyards and hills of Tuscany.

The long table in the informal dining area, right, was originally a local tailor's cutting board. The chairs and credenza are Tuscan antiques. Recently made by a Tuscan artisan, the lacquered wood cupboard, above, was modeled after the credenzas produced in the region during the 17th century. It now stores bright D'Este ceramics, which are crafted near Ferrara.

An exquisite chest in a small sitting room has floral designs and a landscape painted with *tempera magra*, a thin flat watercolor used frequently for decorative patterns in the 1700s to make inexpensive cuts of wood appear richer. This type of decoration was often found in Venetian and Tuscan furniture.

An informal living room, left, includes sofas and chairs covered in a cloverleaf print cotton. The white wood staircase, below, was constructed during the restoration of the farmhouse. Wood floors painted various shades of green bring the tones of the gardens indoors.

White and red velvet-covered chairs in an upstairs bedroom are from the 1700s.

A small stucco building, with a terra-cotta tiled roof, covers a well close to the farmhouse.

A reminder of the villa's earlier origins as a farmhouse is the wood barrel, left, which contains natural fertilizer and has been used on the property since the 19th century. Striped patio chairs create an informal outdoor conversation spot beneath a plant-covered loggia, below.

The 18th-century villa is located in the Brianza countryside near Milan. Gardens are filled with Gianpaolo Porlezza's rare roses, right. From a second-story terrace, far right, one can see the rolling hills of the 50-acre property.

porlezza

COUNTRY RETREAT FILLED WITH COLLECTIONS

The compact villa with its yellow ocher facade and sloping gardens was built in 1750 in the Brianza, a region that lies between Milan and the Alps. It was once owned by an English noblewoman who sided with Italian partisans during their *Risorgimento,* or unification struggle, against Austria in the 1860s. Today, set among gently rolling hills, it is the tranquil weekend and vacation home for Gianpaolo Porlezza, the head of Taroni fabrics, and his wife, Silvana Bernasconi, an editor for *Vogue Italia.*

When they purchased the house 25 years ago, they split design responsibilities—she took the interior, he the gardens. As a noted horticulturist, Porlezza began his cultivation of rare, near-extinct roses. Carefully tended beds containing over 270 species now surround the statue-filled grounds.

The interior could easily have been styled by a well-traveled Renaissance prince: Elaborately carved late Renaissance antiques, ceramics, and sculptures are combined with Oriental furniture, fabrics, and statues. Venetian mosaic floors match the furniture and objects in resplendent detail.

Rooms have their own personal flavor. There's the rustic casualness of the breakfast room/informal dining area, the masculine style of the living area, the South Seas feeling of the second-story studio, the museum-quiet of the painting-lined sitting room. Since the couple travel extensively and are diligent collectors, Signora Porlezza rotates furniture, sometimes storing new purchases for five years until, as she says, "the right moment." Collections abound, among them a constantly expanding assemblage of abstract and futurist art, Russian icons, and perfume boxes from all over the world.

A small dining room has two 16th-century Italian wooden cupids flanking a red-curtained window. The statue is a 16th-century German piece.

The Porlezza villa has many Renaissance antiques. The hand-painted *cassapanca*, or bench, right, is from central Italy. A *cassapanca* frequently stored a family's wealth and was placed in the entrance of a *palazzo* or villa. On the first floor a spacious corridor, below, has a 16th-century Piedmontese sofa and chair and an ornately carved Florentine table. The large wooden religious statue was produced a century later. The flooring is Venetian marble mosaic.

Signora Porlezza likes to collect china, glassware, and informal tableware from all over the world. These red ceramic pieces were made by artisans in Sardinia. The tapestry is from the 16th century.

Elaborately sculpted wood furniture, straight-backed chairs, and marble mosaic flooring create a Renaissance feeling in the dining room, right. The small studio, below, houses many of the Porlezzas' travel finds such as Balinese statues and the Chinese bed topped with five thin silk mattresses, all from the 19th century.

The well-preserved Tudor Gothic chair, from the master bedroom, is accented by an antique petit point throw pillow.

An English painting hangs above the bedroom's 16th-century *cassettone*, or chest of drawers. The mirrors are Italian from the 16th or 17th centuries.

The headboard, which originally was a fireplace mantel, and the bed are Italian pieces from the 16th century and are covered with 18th-century Indian cashmere in a rich paisley design.

The white-and-blue-tiled bathroom provided a perfect spot for the marble-topped table, a Scottish antique that now serves as a *coiffeuse*.

The wooden mannequin, below, is one of a group dating from the 16th and 17th centuries that stands in a foyer. Mannequins of this type were used during the Renaissance by tailors and textile manufacturers for clothing and fabric presentations at court or in the homes of important families. The 16th-century *cassettone*, right, probably from Tuscany or Lombardy, is sculpted in the *bamboccio* or *bambino* style, so named because of the puppet-like or childlike faces and figurines in the carving. Renaissance *cassettone* were often embellished by intricate detailing, which was sometimes religious but more often secular in inspiration.

The chalet, where the Nuvolettis are in residence two months
each winter and part of the
summer, has a pinewood-and-
stone facade, below. At the
entrance, right, a Tyrolean bear
holds a collection of dog
chains. The lighting fixture
above the door is from the
Trentino, one of the northernmost regions of Italy, and was
crafted in the late 19th century.
The sled, hand-painted stool,
and box are from Cortina.

agnelli/nuvoletti

ALPINE CHALET IN THE DOLOMITES

Villa Bella, the winter and summer vacation retreat of Giovanni Nuvoletti and his wife, the former Clara Agnelli, is located in the center of the Dolomite town of Cortina d'Ampezzo. Appropriately Alpine in design, the structure of the house is built along compact chalet like lines with low-beamed ceilings, boiserie-covered walls, and warm topazy light drifting from antique lamps and fireplaces suggest a relaxing winter warmth—laced with colorful Middle-European ac-cents: Austrian and Bohemian can-delabra,chandeliers, lamps, and clocks and German and Hungarian collages and paintings. "Although it's a house in the mountains, I didn't want the interior to be rustic," says Signora Nuvoletti, who planned the interior decor with her husband. "Some say the house has a Russian flavor. Maybe it's true, but this certainly wasn't intended."

Architect Luigi Vietti redesigned the interior, making large rooms out of several smaller ones and creating a feeling of spaciousness not evident when viewing Villa Bella from outside. Since the Nuvolettis entertain a lot and the house is frequently filled with children, grandchildren, nephews, and friends, the living area had to be large and organized into several separate receiving, music, and conversation areas. A gracious mix of antiques— charming examples of local wood craftsmanship from two of the northernmost regions of Italy, the Trentino and Alto Adige, as well as from Bavaria and Bohemia—can be found in this cozy room. A hand-painted pianoforte topped with family photographs stands at its center. The kitchen is frequently used by both Nuvolettis, who are accomplished cooks. "The more elaborate the meal I have to prepare, the better," says Signora Nuvoletti.

Upstairs bedrooms are soft-toned and romantic or reflect an appealing Alpine style with hand-painted beds, chests, and armoires. Terraces for sunbathing overlook the grounds. The house, built in 1935, was purchased by Signora Nuvoletti in the 1950s.

Signor Nuvoletti says that this section of the living area reminds him of a compartment in the Trans-Siberian railway, the train that links Moscow with the Asian coast of the Pacific Ocean. Nineteenth-century Austrian sofas are covered in white deerskin. Windows are trimmed with red velvet curtains and gold *mantovane,* or valances. The large stone tiles are from the region.

In another corner of the large living room, two 19th-century Hungarian portraits hang above the elaborately curved Italian sofa from the 1950s. The carpet is from the surrounding region of Ampezzo and represents a peacock's plumage. It was made with old pieces of fabric that are extensively embroidered and then sewn into the intricate pattern. The center table and pillows were locally crafted, too.

A large hand-painted piano-forte, which is topped with family portraits and Bohemian candelabra, dominates the center of the living area.

A chess set rests on an Italian table whose base was carved during the 17th century, above. An Austrian painting positioned above it hangs on the rusticated stone walls. The 19th-century brierwood table is surrounded by four Biedermeier chairs, above right. The armoire, above far right, was made in Bavaria in 1725. Pieces of antique embroidered velvet, found in a church, hang at each side. The Italian chairs are reproductions of 19th-century models.

A collection of glass and silver vases tops tables and bookshelves outside the dining area, below. The dining table and chandelier, which is still lit by candles, are from the 19th century. The side cupboard, right, was made by local mountain craftsmen and stores Bavarian porcelain, silver service pieces, and figurines.

The kitchen is frequently used by both Nuvolettis, who are accomplished cooks. Table, chairs, cupboards, and copper mugs are all from Cortina.

A small bedroom sitting area, below, is colored in soft pinks and greens. The Italian chaise is from the early 20th century. A pink *salottino*, or little drawing room, right, on the chalet's second level, has abundant old-world charm and a decidedly nonrustic flavor. Swag curtains and a velvet rose-embroidered tablecloth are Italian from the 19th century. One bedroom, far right, has a *baldacchino* bed, which is draped in white eyelet. It was made near Cortina and encompasses a second bed that slips out from underneath.

Delicate frescoes were painted in the bathroom by the contemporary muralist Boccanegra, highly regarded in the Veneto for his exquisite decorative wall treatments.

The guest bedroom has a distinctly Alpine feeling. A colorful cupboard made in the Cortina area displays a row of white 19th-century vases, left. The two hand-painted beds are Austrian, below.

Rows of shuttered windows line the facade of the 18th-century villa in Como, below. A small neo-Gothic *dépendance* hidden by trees serves as guesthouse; a clubhouse and tennis court are located in the hills. Once overgrown, the gardens, now trimmed to formal precision, border the lake, right.

versace

Gardens in disorder, 50-foot-high frescoed ceilings obscured by thick layers of paint, gracious rooms chopped into inelegant smaller spaces—such was the state in which Gianni Versace found the 18th-century Lago di Como villa. But the discovery ended a lengthy search for a weekend getaway and, with customary undauntedness, Versace began the time-consuming renovation project, personally hiring local artisans to recover some of the villa's distinctive attributes. "Each step took months," says Versace. Once he decided to tame the wildly overgrown gardens, there seemed to be as much work to do outside as indoors, and some of Italy's finest landscape gardeners were employed.

Versace refurbished the villa with the help of Francesco Cirincioni, a noted antiquarian. "My apartment in Milan is modern, so I was interested in a complete change from that," he says. "But the style had to be appropriate to the villa, too. And not like a museum; I wanted a mix." He selected a blend of Italian and French antiques from Neoclassic, Direttorio, and Empire periods and embellished them with statuary and grisailles, monochromatic renderings that give the effect of sculpture reliefs.

Versace's own enterprising quests resulted in such special finds as chandeliers and furniture that once belonged to the Bourbon family who ruled Naples in the 19th century. The house's intricate mosaic marble floors, exquisite carpets of stone that had long been covered by large rugs, influenced furniture placement in the major rooms. The swirling patterns of the marble demonstrate what Walter Pater, the 19th-century aesthete, described when referring to the decorative floors in the homes of the ancient Romans, "the real economy that there was in the production of a rich interior effect by a somewhat lavish expenditure upon the surface they trod upon."

The beautiful neoclassically patterned 18th-century marble floor is the main decorative element in the drawing room, furnished sparely with 19th-century Italian and French antiques, far left. The chairs are by Jacob, the renowned cabinetmaker of the French Rococo period. The dining room, left, adjacent to the drawing room, was similarly underfurnished so that the floor mosaics and lakeside views would have a greater impact. The room's Italian mahogany antiques are from the early 19th century. Covering the dining table is an embroidered Pratesi linen tablecloth. A 19th-century Florentine painting is positioned over a commode in the dining room, below left.

Versace's studio, furnished in the country Empire style, provides a welcome escape from his hectic Milan schedule. Nineteenth-century desks are situated at each end of the room.

The Empire-style bed is found in Versace's bedroom on the villa's second floor, below. The bedroom's ruby-and-crystal chandelier, which once belonged to Naples' ruling Bourbon family, is reflected in the mirror, right. The neoclassically styled fireplace is of white marble.

The patterns of the marble mosaic flooring differ from room to room. A star-shaped design decorates the floor in the bedroom belonging to Gianni Versace's sister, Donatella, above. In another corner of the bedroom, a 19th-century folding screen from Lombardy stands near an Empire-style secretaire, right.

A large bathroom adjoins Donatella's bedroom. The marble tub is from the early 19th century; the paintings are from Piedmont.

The master bathroom's cool, blue-gray tones come from *pietra serena* tiles, which have been used for Italian buildings since the Renaissance, particu- larly in Tuscany where they are quarried. The sculpture resting on the tub was inspired by ancient Rome and dates from the 17th century.

Neoclassical grisailles were placed above a beautifully carved Carrara marble bench and the curtained doorway in the master bath.

In one well-lit corridor adjoining a staircase on the first floor, the marble bas-reliefs are from the school of Andrea Appiani, the 19th-century neoclassic Milanese artist who was a favorite of Napoleon.

The entrance foyer, above, includes an 18th-century Tuscan portrait and an Empire-style sofa. One of the villa's marble stairways leads to a hallway, right, with trompe l'oeil frescoes and a 19th-century Roman marble urn and bench.

A prodigious sweep of trompe l'oeil frescoes painted by an anonymous 18th-century artist covers the walls and ceiling of the drawing room, right. The tones are reminiscent of those favored by Tiepolo. Two doors of the main *salone,* far right, open to the garden and flank a console bar and Italian Louis XV chairs.

ferragamo/ san giuliano

SOUVENIRS OF A BAROQUE PAST

The facade of the quattrocento Palazzo Feroni-Magnani is deceptively plain, but the central courtyard with its graceful arches hints at an interior richness of style. One enters the ground-floor apartment, the city base of the Marchese and Marchesa di San Giuliano, through thick wooden Florentine doors and immediately finds an imposing array of frescoes. Painted during the 1700s, they provide the main decorative element of the apartment's splendid rooms. These frescoes sweep the *salone grande* in soft Tiepolo tones: trompe l'oeil portals topped by balustrades frame doors, swirls of clouds and an angel-encircled Diana make the tall, vaulted ceiling seem limitless. The frescoes in the dining area are more linear, depicting Tuscan architectural elements, while those on the ceilings of the bedrooms portray a range of allegorical scenes. Additional embellishment is supplied by the gilt-leaf borders on the bedroom entrance arch, and a theater frontispiece, an example of ornate baroque stuccowork, adorning the opening to the children's rooms.

Since the drawing room frescoes were the most elaborate in the apartment, clean-lined modern pieces were chosen to furnish the room and dramatize the beauty and grandeur of the art-covered walls and ceilings with contemporary simplicity. Italian antiques, as well as some French and English pieces, all dating from the 17th to 19th centuries can be found throughout the other rooms and add appropriate old-world touches to the graceful ambience that readily summons forth images from a baroque past.

An 18th-century Italian chandelier, a bouquet of crystal and gilt-bronze that is a San Giuliano family heirloom, lights a formally appointed dining room. The English candelabra are from the 19th century. Frescoes in this room depict Tuscan architectural elements.

The family monogram is etched in a set of crystal goblets, which are part of the understated, elegant table set by the marchesa. The antique damask cloth is from Sicily and embroidered with the family monogram, above. Ginori china in the "Viscount" pattern was chosen to complement the elegant and unfussy lines of the silver-and-vermeil flatwear. Individual wine decanters are placed at each setting, above right.

In the *biblioteca*, or library, a
17th-century Venetian *coro*,
once a choir stall, above, now
serves as a U-shaped bookcase
that runs along three of the
library walls. The Italian settee
based on a French model, right,
is walnut trimmed and dates
from the 18th century. The
fresco on the library ceiling, far
right, depicts the Villa Bella-
vista, the summer residence of
the Feroni family, original
inhabitants of the Florentine
palazzo in which the San Giuliano apartment is located.

One of the two ceiling frescoes in the master bedroom portrays an allegory of justice.

An ornamented arch trimmed with *sfoglia dorata,* or gilt-leaf borders, and topped with molding divides the large master bedroom in two zones. The alcove was probably once a music room; immediately outside is a small sitting area.

The courtyard, left and below, a tranquil contrast to the frenetic scene on nearby Florentine streets, includes a long arcade dotted with classically inspired statues from the 18th and 19th centuries.

The Palazzo Feroni-Magnani was built during the *quattrocento,* the 1400s, and the early Renaissance rule of Lorenzo de' Medici. It reflects the Florentine architectural style of restrained grandeur. The massive oak doors, above, at the entrance to the ground-floor apartment, are typical of those found in many Florentine *palazzi.*

The intarsia wood chair, right, produced in Syria during the 19th century, is located in the master bedroom; the painting is part of Signora Porlezza's collection of children's portraits. Arranged atop an ivory/mother-of-pearl *cassettone*, far right, is a collection of cloisonné vases.

porlezza

SMALL-SCALE LUXURY FOR AN APARTMENT

When you're a collector and like to display the art and antiques you've gathered over the years, a small apartment that's difficult to furnish under any circumstances can present a particular problem. The Porlezzas who, as shown, have a large villa close to Milan, didn't want anything more than a *pied-à-terre* for their city base; yet it had to accommodate some of their paintings, tapestries, Renaissance antiques, and furniture, as well as be comfortable enough for frequent weekday evening dinner parties.

The apartment has a linear arrangement of small rooms. The combination living room/study, the dining room, and the master bedroom on one side of the corridor all have large windows looking on to busy Milanese streets; the kitchen and baths are directly opposite the public rooms. To make the public rooms and bedroom appear more spacious than they are, walls were removed and replaced by sliding partitions, which when open create a flowing loftlike expanse with ample room for guests.

Most of the furnishings were carefully edited from the Porlezzas' substantial collection of antiques so as not to overpower the apartment's small dimensions. When none of the antiques seemed right for the tiny living room/study, a contemporary Italian sofa, ottoman, chair, and black lacquered table were selected. The modern red lacquered bookcases were designed by Signora Porlezza.

Walls and sliding panels were covered with paintings, bookshelves were dotted with Oriental objects, and tabletops filled with antique bronzes and assorted figurines. But in a small apartment, space quickly runs out, so Signora Porlezza placed several antique urns on the floor and tucked Renaissance wooden statues into the corners.

Painted with *succo di erba,* or vegetable dyes, instead of being handwoven, the type of Renaissance tapestry on the wall in the corridor often depicted mythological or religious subjects. The settee, upholstered in white fabric, has rungs carved a *rocchetto,* in spoollike shapes, which is a style characteristic of Italian chairs, beds, and tables made from the 15th to 17th centuries.

Three rooms of the apartment are separated by sliding panels; the one between the dining and living area has canvases on either side. Large win- dows overlooking a busy section of downtown Milan con- tribute a sense of spaciousness. The lacquered table and sofas are modern Italian pieces.

The only pieces of furniture in the dining room are the 16th-century oak table and chairs carved *a rocchetto*. A 19th-century Italian tapestry is displayed on one wall.

Signora Porlezza's collection of children's paintings completely cover the walls of the master bedroom. They are by Italian, French, and English artists and date from the 16th to 18th centuries.

Signora Porlezza designed the bookcases along contemporary lines and painted them her favorite bright red. She added the 17th-century Italian chair covered with tapestry for a contrast of texture and style.

Japanese, Chinese, and Indian figurines and vases from the Porlezzas' extensive travels rest on the studio's bookcases, right. An 18th-century Italian portrait hangs over the desk. The brightly lacquered teapot, below, was found in the Orient.

I L M O D E

The concept of modern style has changed in recent years as Italians seek to add new warmth to their homes. Interior design schemes have become less restrictive and more personal, without necessarily broadening to include antiques. The innovative furniture and lighting created by some of Italy's leading architects immediately after the Second World War remained popular during the 1960s and 1970s. Indeed, these sofas, chairs, tables, and lighting designs are still used in a wide range of interiors, from urban apartments to country villas. But pieces from the early 20th-century movements like *floreale,* or Art Nouveau, and Art Deco, as well as furniture from the Wiener Werkstätte and reissues of classic Bauhaus designs, have appealed to an increasing number of Italians, whose flair for mixing styles has proved to be as genial with contemporary pieces as it has been with antiques.

Sculpture from the early 20th century is displayed throughout the Ricci town house. A piece by Guiraud Rivière, right, the 1920s sculptor, is prominently placed in the living room. Two vases, one French from the 1920s, the other Murano glass, flank the work by the Art Deco sculptor Chiparus, far right.

ricci

A DIFFERENT KIND OF EARLY MODERN

"It's in continuous evolution," says Franco Maria Ricci, the fine-arts book and magazine publisher, of his pair of attached *palazzi* on the outskirts of Milan. He oversaw the five-year restoration of the late 19th-century structures feeling that "architects all do the same things." Connected by an elevator, the three stories, including one underground, are all multilevel, compensating for the unaligned floors of the pair of attached town houses.

An eclectic style prevails throughout—one dominated by furniture from the early masters of modern design. A Thonet console and mirror greet visitors in the entrance vestibule, Hoffmann chairs are positioned in the library and in the corridors, and a simple Ruhlmann bed and chairs are located in one of the bedrooms. When the appropriate sofa or chair couldn't be found, Ricci designed his own, usually in a style inspired by Art Deco. But the furniture includes a few antiques and contemporary pieces as well—a prized 18th-century table that once belonged to the gran duchessa Maria Luigia of Parma, Napoleon's second wife, and black lacquered bookcases that were produced within the last few years.

Wall colors depart dramatically from the white so often used in Italian interiors. Known for his dramatic color sense, Ricci chose to have his living and dining rooms painted lobster red, and bedroom aqua, and he had the wallpaper for the office and entrance vestibule specially made to reproduce a lush floral design from a Gobelin tapestry. The unexpected colors provide a striking backdrop to the highly personal assemblage of furniture, art, and sculpture in the Milanese town house that has become the perfect home for the gentlemanly aesthete, whose taste Diana Vreeland, special consultant to the Metropolitan Museum of Art in New York, once described as totally foreign to the American eye.

Painted black in a row of white facades, the two small *palazzi* were linked to create spacious living quarters. The windows, part of the houses' original structure, were styled after 18th-century English models.

The dining room and library open to the garden, where Ricci keeps two large turtles and a fox terrier. The exterior of the house is covered with ivy and overgrown shrubs. Potted red geraniums add a dash of color.

When not designing his own pieces, Ricci collects furniture from early modern masters. A small sitting area near the living room has a Hoffmann chair and, to its right, a Thonet table, and Chiparus statues, above. The lobster red living room, left, includes sofas that Ricci designed. The painting of the tiger is by the Italian artist Ligabue, the subject of one of the books Ricci published.

In Ricci's home office a painting by Ligabue is positioned over a desk and Thonet chair, below. Black lacquered cabinets from the early 20th century are used for storage. A beautiful antique lace curtain, right, graces the office window. The wallpaper pattern in the office and entrance foyer, far right, was based on a Gobelin tapestry design. The mirror and console are Thonet pieces.

The lace curtain, above, is woven in a typical 19th-century Italian pattern. Contemporary black lacquered bookcases, right, have mirrored panels with designs that repeat those of the Hoffmann chairs. Shelves are filled with many of Ricci's silk-bound editions.

In another section of the library, a rare edition of the drawings of Giovanni Battista Piranesi, the Italian painter and engraver whose books helped spur the revival of interest in antiquity during the 1700s, rests atop an Italian table from the 18th century.

An unusual mix of materials contributes to the highly original bathroom, below. The mirrored tiles on the walls contrast with the black tiles lining the marble-rimmed tub. The statue perched on the bathtub rim is by Chiparus, right.

Antique Delft china, used for informal meals, is arranged on the marble-topped table in the bright skylighted dining area, right. The painting is by Domenico Gnoli, a contemporary Italian neofigurative artist, and the five statues, below, often positioned at the center of the dining table, are by Chiparus (the first three from left), Zach, and Barthélemy.

The verdant inner courtyard of the Palazzo Taverna, below, leads to Graziella Lonardi's house. Her gallery is located in another part of the *palazzo*. A glass-enclosed passageway links the living area with the bedrooms, right. An easel bears a saying of the Swiss artist Ben Vautier: "To change art one must change man."

lonardi

LIVING WITH ART IN A 13TH-CENTURY PALAZZO

The setting couldn't be more Roman: a residence in the antique 13th-century fortress, the Palazzo Taverna, once owned by the Borghese family; glass-topped cupolas, terra-cotta tiled roofs, a lush patio-garden. It is the Rome-based home/studio/salon of Graziella Lonardi, one of the city's foremost art dealers. "My home life and work are completely integrated," says Signora Lonardi, whose gallery is in the same *palazzo*. "My work is a way of living." She entertains frequently with lunches and dinners, bringing together an international mix of artists, directors, actors, and art collectors.

Floor-to-ceiling glass windows line an art-filled entranceway linking bedrooms to the main drawing room. Cupolas with skylights define several rooms, two of which are embellished with specially designed sculpture and paintings. Beneath the enormous living room skylight, Signora Lonardi has created a "winter garden" of hanging plants. The furniture she designed in conjunction with Terry Vaina, a Roman interior designer, is simple: chairs and sofas upholstered in inexpensive canvas, glass tables supported by antique stone capitals, large cushions for patio seating. "I wanted the furniture to form a backdrop to and not compete with the art," says Signora Lonardi. Her collection consists predominantly of the work of Italian postwar contemporary and avant-garde artists such as Lucio Fontana, Renato Guttuso, Vettor Pisani, Michelangelo Pistoletto, Alberto Burri, and Alighiero Boetti, as well as pieces by Cy Twombly and Andy Warhol.

Glass-topped cupolas form skylights in several rooms. A wire sculpture by Luciano Fabro, an Italian conceptualist, was created for the space.

A small foyer, below, connects the entrance to the living area. The painting above the door and the sculpture in the left niche are by Lucio Fontana; the palette was designed by Vettor Pisani. Andy Warhol's portrait of Signora Lonardi, right, located in the living room, can be seen through the door, below.

Signora Lonardi's "winter garden" hangs from a grid that spans the opening of one of the glass-topped cupolas, left. Comfortable sofas, covered in canvas, flank the door which opens on to the courtyard. An antique Russian samovar dominates a low glass table. Renato Guttuso sketched a portrait of Signora Lonardi on a wall, above. She paired it with one of his paintings placed in a niche.

The dining table, devised by Terry Vaina and Signora Lonardi, has a base made from antique stone capitals. Positioned on the wall directly behind the table is Cy Twombly's *Blackboard*. The candelabra are English.

The atrium, below, has a glass covering, which creates a greenhouse environment during the winter months in which bougainvillea, oleander, hibiscus, mimosa, palm, and olive trees can flourish. The high-gloss tiles, which look black when wet, are actually dark green and are from the Sorrento area. A brightly colored Saporiti chair called "Miamina," right, picks up the tones of the flowering garden plants.

saporiti

AN ATRIUM IN THE SUBURBS

The villa was to be airy and open, yet private; spacious although confined to one level. Built in the late 1970s for Giorgio Saporiti, the head of Saporiti International, the contemporary furniture manufacturer, and his family, the exterior of the house designed by the architect Vittorio Introini is rationalist in inspiration. Its interior layout follows a classic Mediterranean model: a square of rooms that face an atrium. The atrium is topped by a sliding glass covering shaped like a cupola that creates a greenhouse for an assortment of flowering plants.

The floor-to-ceiling glass walls of the living area afford a striking view of the atrium with its deep green tiles, lush green plants, vibrantly colored bougainvillea and azalea, life-sized wood sculpture, and pastel-toned chairs. Long corridors furnished simply with white consoles and accented by modern paintings and sculpture flank the three other sides of the atrium, each corridor opening to a separate zone of the house: kitchen, dining area, and breakfast room; master bedroom and bath; and children's rooms. Like many contemporary suburban villas, the Saporiti home was designed to capture as much of the daylight as possible and to maximize views of the grounds. All of the rooms along the exterior have large glass windows facing on to the terrace, which has been planted with shrubbery.

The interior decor planned by Saporiti represents the relaxed contemporary style popular in Italy during the late 1960s and early 1970s. Furniture is functional, clean-lined, sometimes gently curved, and often slightly oversized, with table surfaces of glass or high-gloss lacquer, upholstery fabric usually muted, and color coming from the modern art or from Missoni-designed tapestries and carpets.

Dark tiles make the pink of the Saporiti chairs seem more vibrant. The wood statue, *Amanti,* is the work of contemporary Italian sculptor Tavenari.

Horizontal in line, rationalist in inspiration, the villa, built in the late 1970s, has only one floor but a spacious interior, above. The house is surrounded by a tiled patio and rimmed with plants that create a visual link with those found in other parts of the property, above right. The pastel pink chair and lime green bowls, right, were selected to harmonize with the atrium's colorful plants and flowers. The bowls are by Bernini and made of Murano glass.

The living room, below right, which faces the atrium, is expansive, yet simply furnished. Sofas and chairs are called "Onda" (Wave), and were designed by Giovanni Offredi for Saporiti International. A Missoni rug adds a patchwork of color. Carpet and sofas, below, have a velvety texture and muted gray-green tone.

Lacquered table surfaces and white high-gloss walls contribute to a bright environment. The rotating crystal sculpture is by Matteuzzi.

The table on the veranda of the Missonis' house, right, is laid with a light luncheon buffet. The veranda, where the family and their guests usually dine, is glass-enclosed and overlooks acres of luscious gardens. The chairs, covered in Missoni fabric, are from the 18th century. A simple wood table and director's chairs, far right, accommodate extra guests in another corner of the veranda.

missoni

BRILLIANT SCHEMES FOR A ONE-LEVEL RETREAT

"When you have a kitchen, bathroom, and bedroom, you have a home," says Tai Missoni. While there's considerably more than this to the Missoni home in Varese, a town near Milan, the one-level structure does reflect both Tai and Rosita's directness and fondness for an uncomplicated style. Their house is surrounded by acres of gardens filled with oak, birch, chestnut, and ash trees, fruit arbors, a pool, and family pets —even chickens and hens. The Missoni knitwear factory is located a few steps away from the property.

"I don't like architects telling me where to eat and to live," says Tai, who worked with architect Arigo Buzzi on the floor plans. Informality is the key: The Missonis prefer to dine on the glass-enclosed veranda rather than in the more formal dining room. There is always a place for more guests at the table: children with their spouses, members of the extended Missoni business "family," and overseas clients.

Throughout the walls are painted white. "It's the simplest color," says Tai. "I find anything else limits you. Nature gives you all you need, particularly if you live in the middle of the woods as we do." One can find a Missoni imprimatur in each of the rooms. Color comes from the brilliant mosaic and patchwork fabric patterns the Missonis design for chairs, sofas, and pillows, and from the collages for which Tai is the creative director.

Even if the house is in constant evolution, major changes are rare. Collections may expand, baskets and pottery from Tai and Rosita's worldwide travels may be rearranged, new fabrics added, but the effect remains always and uniquely Missoni.

The entrance to the suburban villa, right, includes a tiled walkway bordered by plants and flowers, and an oversized Missoni logo stretching the length of an exterior wall. Surrounded by trees and gardens, center right, the house is a few steps away from the Missoni factory. There's also a pool, far right, a tennis court, and even a small barnyard on the property.

The Missoni house is accented by the sculpture, figurines, boxes, and fabric they collect from all over the world. The still lifes that appear throughout the villa are characterized by the Missonis' sense of color and design, left and below.

Most of the rooms feature large windows that frame the surrounding landscape. In the spacious living area, the rug and the fabrics covering sofas and pillows were designed by the Missonis.

Adding a humorous touch to the bright, modern kitchen is the spaghetti sculpture found by the Missonis' youngest son, Luca, in a restaurant in Tokyo.

Baskets and other objects collected during the family's travels are arranged on a Tuscan table, left, which dates from the 16th century. The carpet is a Missoni design. Ceramic mosaics color a 19th-century *comodino*, or night table, and a small vase, which are located near the villa's entrance foyer, below.

Like many lakeside houses built in Italy during the middle of the 19th century, the three-story villa, right, is rectangular in shape and has large high-ceilinged rooms. One side of the villa faces Lago di Como, far right, the other acres of formal gardens.

fasana

OPULENCE AND ART DECO BY THE LAKE

I t is a house that summons images from a leisurely past, of lunches in verdant, expansive gardens, of receiving friends who travel a luminous lake by boat, of summers that linger into early fall. Completed in 1860 by architect Giacomo Bassi for Count Giulio Belinzaghi, then the mayor of Milan, the three-floor villa rests on the shores of Lago di Como, next to the internationally known Villa d'Este and within an hour's drive of downtown Milan.

Giorgio Fasana, owner of Setarium, a major Italian textiles firm, and his wife, Paola, who purchased the house in 1981, felt it would be a mistake to fill the large, airy rooms with furniture from the period in which the villa was built. Rather than what they considered to be the inevitable heaviness of Napoleon III, they opted for Italian and French Art Deco pieces from the 1930s and 1940s, complemented by contemporary furniture as well as a few 19th-century Chinese antiques.

Art Deco furniture is strikingly displayed against the villa's silk-lined walls, particularly in the all-white drawing rooms. More vibrant tones of rust, red, and vermilion characterize second-level bedrooms. Marble fireplaces, delicate stuccowork on door lintels and ceilings, and exquisite frescoes in the bathroom are reminders of the villa's 19th-century origins.

The Fasanas chose to keep the walls as spare and uncluttered as possible, particularly the public rooms on the main floor, where floor-to-ceiling windows open to dramatic lake views. An extraordinary heliocoid stairway links the ground floor with the second and third levels. Beneath the villa, the *imbarcadero,* or landing stage, houses the small motor launch the Fasanas use for jaunts to nearby villas.

A black lacquered table with chairs in the Chinese Chippendale style made by a Como artisan, below, are positioned on a terrace running along the villa's first level and facing the lake. A pair of Art Deco chairs viewed from a first-floor window and a ceramic panther standing on a mirrored tabletop are silhouetted against a backdrop of Lago di Como, right.

The Fasanas' motor launch, right, is stored in the *imbarcadero*, located beneath the villa.

The cast-iron statue, left, discovered in the *imbarcadero*, once stood watch in a Venetian port and now presides over the dining room. Wanting to emphasize the airiness and grandeur of the public rooms, the Fasanas lined all the walls and framed the entrance and passageway between the living and dining rooms with ivory Italian silk, above.

The lacquered Chinese dining table and the Italian chairs fashioned after 19th-century Chinese models are offset against the light walls and floor in the dining room, below, where furniture was positioned for symmetrical balance. The chandelier is Italian from the 19th century.

A white and ivory *salotto* has a fresh Art Deco flavor, below. The pendulum clock is by Ruhlmann; the Italian chairs are from the 1930s.

As there were few comfortably upholstered sofas made in Italy during the 1930s and 1940s when Art Deco was popular, the Fasanas decided to add contemporary versions covered in ivory Italian silk, above. Most Art Deco chairs and sofas, whether French or Italian in origin, were generally constructed to be close to the floor; as a result, accent tables had to be lower, and the coffee or cocktail table as we know it now came into being. The one between the sofas was made in brierwood during the 1930s. The marble fireplace is from the 19th century; the mirror was recently produced.

The Italian mahogany *torchère*, or hall lamp, right, is from the 1930s and stands near the entrance to the dining room. The curved-arm Art Deco chairs are covered in silk and accented with leopard-skin-patterned pillows.

A thick glass table made in Italy during the 1930s, right, with a mirrored and lacquered wood base, holds a vase from the same period and a school of silverfish figurines. Lattice-patterned silk lines walls in the white drawing room, below, which was once a winter garden. Sofas, chair, and cocktail table are contemporary Italian pieces. A large 19th-century Italian painting hangs above a sofa.

The oval-shaped master bathroom was beautifully painted with frescoes during the 19th century. Its floor and tub are of an unusually deep blue-green marble.

A heliocoid stairway links the villa's three levels. A table displaying 19th-century sculpture and vases is positioned at its base.

In the entrance foyer, Italian chairs based on 19th-century Chinese models rest on either side of a black lacquered commode. The white ceramic porcelain bear is by Lejean.

Vermilion-colored Italian silk with a print inspired by an antique Chinese pattern was used for bedroom curtains, chairs, and dressing table, below. *Bauli*, or large trunks, with Oriental-style handles provide additional storage space. A portrait of a Chinese family interpreted in Italian silk is positioned above the bed's headboard, left.

The swirling lines of the banister's grille contrast with the straight-backed square-armed Italian chairs made during the 1930s. A porcelain-and-quartz fish sculpture rests on a brier-wood table.

Shaded by a large canvas umbrella, the patio adjacent to the villa, below, is used daily during the summer for informal meals. The umbrella is by Vivai del Sud. A wood walkway surrounds the large pool in the back of the house, right.

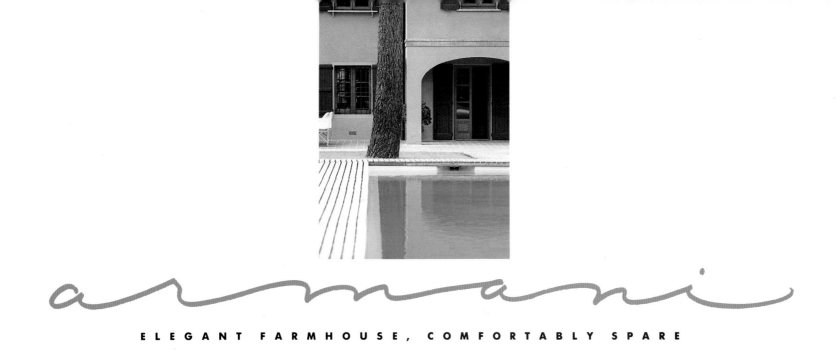

armani

When Giorgio Armani purchased the Forte dei Marmi *cascina,* or farmhouse, which had been converted into a large vacation home in 1940, he decided against using the country-style furnishings that the house seemed to suggest. Armani designs the interiors of all his residences—an apartment in Milan and another vacation spot in the south of Italy—adhering to a style that incorporates a clean-lined sophisticated simplicity with modern comfort.

The interior space was completely reorganized, rooms gutted and new wall and floor coverings installed. Aluminum paneling and straw matting were repeated throughout the house for continuity. Each of the floors is multilevel and staggered so that the mansard attic beams are visible from the ground floor. Armani organized the living area into a winter and summer zone. The winter zone is accented by a fireplace and fur rug, the summer area, which opens on to the garden and patio, by large cotton-covered divans and chairs. All furniture was designed by Armani with the exception of his white studio desk, a Hoffmann piece dating from 1911, and the Italian dining table and chairs from the 1930s.

The house has a tranquil orderliness, a precise place-for-everything scheme, and a geometric harmony that provides a soothing, relaxing environment. The inspiration for some of the decor was in part Japanese. The idea for the graduated set of amber-toned wooden drawers that forms the base of the stairway between first and second levels was "robbed," Armani says, from a Japanese magazine, as was the multilevel layout.

Wanting to bring "some life to the staircase," Armani created one that was beautiful and extremely functional. Wooden drawers provide storage and in addition serve as the base of the stairway. Triangular lamps were designed by Armani.

There are two living areas in the villa. The summer zone, above, includes large linear divans, which were created by Armani and covered in khaki cotton. In the winter *soggiorno*, left, the look is more intimate, with a fur rug, red lamps, and smaller-scaled furniture contributing to the mood.

A collection of modern copperware decorates one wall of the villa's kitchen, above. White Ginori china and simple English flatware compose an appropriately spare table setting, left, for the dining room.

Paneled in white aluminum, the dining room is geometric in line and completely devoid of clutter. Table and chairs were made in Italy during the 1930s and are among the oldest pieces of furniture in the house.

The white marble bas-relief from Carrara, above, located on one of the house's exterior walls, depicts fishermen, hunters, and cupids. Although its exact origins are unknown, the sculpture was probably crafted in Tuscany during the 19th century. The eagles, left, are also from the 1800s. They were found in a Roman garden and now watch a quiet corner of the Forte dei Marmi grounds.

A small studio was created near the master bedroom. The white desk is a Hoffmann piece from 1911, the lamp an Armani design. The arc-shaped window, which is trimmed in wood, faces on to the garden.

Built along rationalist architectural lines, the villa, below and right, is located in the Emilia-Romagna region of Italy. The bronze sculpture by Jorge Piqueras climbs one of the property's north walls, far right.

cremonesi

A REVIVAL OF 1930S RATIONALISM

The elements are pure 1930s Italian Rationalism: dramatic architectural lines, visible pilasters, tubular railings, a ribbon of horizontal windows, a protuberant balcony. Located near Piacenza and the river Trebbia, where Hannibal defeated the Romans, the house surrounded by forest is the weekend and vacation home of Mario and Lella Cremonesi. It was designed by architect Sandro Masera, who began work on the project in 1974 and completed it three years later.

Beneath the unbroken blue skies of Emilia-Romagna, a region in north central Italy, the house is a gleam of white, with rooftops and terraces trimmed by trees and shrubbery. The north side of the grounds is totally enclosed by walls, ensuring privacy, even for the climbing bronze visitor by Jorge Piqueras. The living, dining, and game rooms are organized on three levels, each linked by a small set of stairs and, like all the other rooms in the house, face south on to a sweep of lawn. The bedrooms and kitchen are bright, spacious, and functional. Furniture by prominent Italian designers—Gae Aulenti, Vico Magistretti, Gaetano Pesce, Tobia Scarpa, Giò Ponti—is rationalist in spirit and marked by a simple, coherent style. A large collection of futurist art is displayed throughout the house.

A white console, below, topped with silver sculpture from the 1920s by Franz and Karl Hagenauer, separates the dining area from the first level of the living room. The rounded shelf is part of a freestanding fireplace. It holds a black sculpture by Pietro Cascella, and a multicolored vase by Rometti, an innovative Italian ceramic artisan from the 1930s.

The "Wink" chair with its Mickey Mouse ears, by Cassina, adds a splash of color to the living room, below. The wheeled glass coffee table holding sculpture by Hagenauer is a Gae Aulenti design. Simple slat stairs lead to the game room, right. The painting is by the futurist M. G. Del Monte.

An enormous glass wall facing on to the garden helps make the small dining room appear more spacious. The table and chairs are Le Corbusier reproductions by Cassina. The thin sliver of a lamp called "Bip Bip" was created by Achille Castiglioni for Flos.

In the dining area an abstract painting by Tullio Catalano hangs near a sliding glass door that frames an indoor garden. Steps lead to the living room on the lower level and to an upstairs game room.

Bordered by a light blue metal railing, the game room, above, includes a sofa by Gaetano Pesce called "Sunset in New York." The modular units vary in height and were designed to convey the feeling of a Manhattan skyline, the large red-orange pillow an evening sunset. The spiral staircase, left, connects the terrace outside the upper-level game room with the roof garden.

An impressionistic view of surrounding trees can be seen through the translucent shades that cover the sloping window. The card table is accompanied by "Spaghetti" chairs, so called because of their thin tubular framework. The silver horse sculpture is by Hagenauer.

The terrace, painted a deep Pompeian red, overlooks Capri's Marina Grande and the Bay of Naples. The statue, below, is from the early 19th century. A crest of the Principi d'Assia, owners of the villa, adorns a wall, right.

Lonardi

Villa Mura is built into steep cliffs, overlook facades and white the Marina Grande, the Bay sparkling thread of coastline. 1930s, the villa has distinct ties dates from the 14th century and times. The villa belongs to the of the Italian royal family; it is nardi, the Roman art dealer island for part of the year from

one of Capri's staggeringly ing villages of chalky plaster cupola roofs. Below there's of Naples, and, at night, a Although constructed in the with the past: Its central tower its outside walls from ancient Principi d'Assia, close relatives now rented by Graziella Lo- who is an active hostess on the spring to early fall.

Because property is at ground scarce, many of the the mountainside. As a result, twisting, usually narrow, are dwellings as their white stucco

a premium in Capri and level houses are built vertically into numerous stairways, often as characteristic of these exteriors. Villa Mura is no

exception: The two-level structure that contains the living area and four bedrooms is linked to the medieval tower by a small set of stairs. The patio at the entrance to the villa serves as an outdoor dining area and is a lively botanical mix of Mediterranean shrubs, citrus trees, and bright red geraniums.

Signora Lonardi kept most of the Italian brierwood furniture from the late 1930s and 1940s that she found in the villa, covering some of the more time-faded sofas and chairs in heavy white cotton. She added her own special assortment of paintings from Italian and German modern and avant-garde artists to each of the rooms.

Capri has been a resort since the time of Emperor Augustus, and classical busts, figurines, vases, and bronzes in the villa's large entrance hall, as well as the Pompeian-red terrace with its statue-filled niche, act as reminders of the island's Roman past.

Planted with local Caprese shrubs and *settembrini,* small flowers that bloom in September, jasmine, and hydrangea, the patio is a fragrant spot for outdoor entertaining, particu-larly aromatic during the eve-ning. A trellis made from tree branches links the white stucco columns. Pavement is of sun-bleached brick arranged in a herringbone pattern.

Windowpanes and framework, painted in aqua, add color to the white stucco exterior. The bust is from a Roman statue.

The fireplace mantel in the living room is topped with Gallé lamps and vases and antique silver mugs, above. Assorted watercolors and landscapes of Capri cover one corridor wall and fill the space above a small writing desk, left. Desk and chairs are Italian from the 1930s.

Chairs from the 1940s were updated with a new covering of heavy white cotton, left. On the wall is a canvas by Mindendoff, a German avant-garde painter.

Bright red anthurium, a French Art Deco-style vase, and a small plaque by Tano Festa, a contemporary Italian artist, which reads, "This is the place of the Gioconda" (Mona Lisa), form a simple still life in one bedroom, below.

The master bedroom, above and right, once belonged to Principessa Mafalda di Savoia. The bed, desk, and chairs are in brierwood and are from the 1930s. Hanging above the bed, which is covered with an English floral print spread, is a drawing by Picasso.

Used as an office by Signora Lonardi when away from her Rome art gallery, the studio in the 14th-century tower is sunny and comfortable. Arc-shaped windows provide spectacular views of the Bay of Naples. Paintings and drawings by Grosz, Klimt, Dix, and Rodin are arranged on the wall behind the canvas-covered chaise longue.

In another corner of the studio, above right, there's a small rush-seated chair and work by a group of Italian and German contemporary avant-garde artists: Michelangelo Pistoletto, Alberto Burri, Lucio Fontana, and Joseph Beuys. Vases and plates crafted in southern Italy are displayed on the sill of a small window that overlooks the garden, right.

Clean-lined modern furniture predominates in the suburban Milanese apartment. The high-backed, softly curving chair, designed by Isozaki for I.C.F., is paired with Zanotta's "Cumano" table, which is covered in white linen and holds a Fontana Arte lamp, right. The geometric "Vanessa" bed in aqua lacquered metal was designed by Tobia Scarpa for Knoll International and was chosen to balance the painting by the Italian futurist Giacomo Balla, located above it, far right.

arosio

Apartments are often more generously proportioned and usually easier to find outside Italy's major urban centers. Even so, Roberto Arosio, a furniture manufacturer whose business is located in a small town in the suburbs near Milan, considered himself fortunate to obtain an apartment above his office headquarters. The space was sizable enough to accommodate an extensive collection of modern art and a growing family.

The Studio Masters of Lissone, a local architectural group, designed the interior, installing and creating rooms that are bathed in natural light. The living room is enormous compared to today's average Italian apartment and was planned to include most of Arosio's major sculpture and art pieces, particularly the full-sized 1930s pop racer, as well as to incorporate a spacious conversation zone. The use of glass walls to line corridors and enclose the small indoor gardens that separate the dining area from the study and the kitchen from the bedrooms makes the rooms in the center of the apartment seem larger than they are.

Modern furniture was chosen to complement the art, resulting in a mix of International Style classics by Le Corbusier, Eero Saarinen, and Mies van der Rohe and contemporary pieces from leading Italian architects and industrial designers such as Mario Bellini, Vico Magistretti, and Carlo Scarpa. The furniture was also selected for its suitability to young children, and many of the pieces in the apartment have uncomplicated lines, durable upholstery fabrics, and rounded surfaces. Arosio oversaw the placement of the furniture, as well as that of the paintings and sculpture. His art collection is constantly changing, as it is rearranged or loaned to artist friends for exhibitions.

The kitchen, although compact, appears spacious because of the glass walls, one of which faces an indoor garden, the other the apartment's central corridor.

The dining room has an uncluttered, unified look, which Arosio achieved by editing the furniture to include only pieces of streamlined design and limiting tones to black and white.

The round table was designed by Eero Saarinen for Knoll International; the chairs were created by Mario Bellini for Cassina; the sideboard is a Vico Magistretti design for Poggi.

The living room, above, includes a large conversation zone at one end, a small sitting area composed of blue-and-orange Cassina chairs near the bookcases, and space enough for the 1930s racer by Salvatore Scarpitta, an Italian pop artist. The Italian fascination for the American West is reflected in the whimsical "Wild West" screen, right, designed by Ugo Nespolo, the Italian neofigurative artist. A cowboy hat and miniature covered wagon serve as an unusual centerpiece on the table draped with an orange cotton tablecloth. Chairs covered in checked fabric are by George Nelson for I.C.F.

A cloud-shaped mirror and sky-blue tiles add a fanciful touch in the master bedroom.

The long central corridor, right, divides the kitchen from the dining room and the living room at the entrance to the apartment from the bedroom section in the back. Glass walls are framed by brushed aluminum strips. Called *Piedi,* or feet, the glass structure attached to the ceiling with a tube of white fabric is by the Italian conceptualist Luciano Fabro. It is located in the studio, which opens on to a small interior garden, center right. The studio, far right, includes a table, chairs, stools, and shelves designed by Le Corbusier. When not in use the worktable holds a display of knives from around the world.

An unusual mix of art and furniture defines the entrance, below. The bust is classically inspired, the vase dates from the Art Deco period, and the tall fish tooth is from a narwhal. Made in the Rajasthan, India, the settee was sculpted in white marble. The stairway, right, is elaborately baroque. Frescoes are from the 18th century, the marble banister added a century later.

tivioli

RIGOROUS LINES, COOL-TONED SYMMETRY

The neighborhood is one of Milan's oldest, where buildings are separated by narrow cobblestoned streets. The *palazzo* is exactly what one would expect to find here—dating from the 17th century with a tiled and columned courtyard, baroque banister, and frescoed entrance. What does come as a surprise, though, is the elegantly rigorous modern interior of fur couturier Carlo Tivioli's apartment.

Under the direction of Turin-based architect Toni Cordero, two floors of the *palazzo* were completely gutted, two new levels were built then linked by a network of metallic stairs and a blue and green color scheme. Rooms were organized in a traditional way: public rooms on the ground floor, private rooms above. The modern furniture includes pieces designed by Cordero as well as reproductions of modern classics by Mies van der Rohe and Le Corbusier. Antiques such as the white marble settee, statues of Hercules and Minerva, 17th-century Italian paintings, and an exquisitely detailed *capo d'opera,* a miniature model for planning an architectural work or piece of furniture, act as counterpoints to the streamlined interior design. The work of post–World War II Italian abstract and avant-garde artists is displayed in most of the rooms.

The dense crowding of *palazzi* in this central Milan district can make abundant daylight an extremely precious commodity. To avoid a gloomy interior, enormous windows were designed for the living room with additional brightness supplied by rectangular translucent panels built into the walls and illuminated by artificial light.

Tivioli finds the modern interior a "perfect environment. It readily adapts to change, to the range of my moods, and to the inclusion of antiques and new works of art I find."

In the living room white canvas-covered sofas by Toni Cordero contrast with the Mies van der Rohe daybed, the Eileen Gray rug "Blackboard," and the granite pavement. Floor lamps by Noguchi add diffused light. The lacquered glass table in the center of the room was also designed by Cordero.

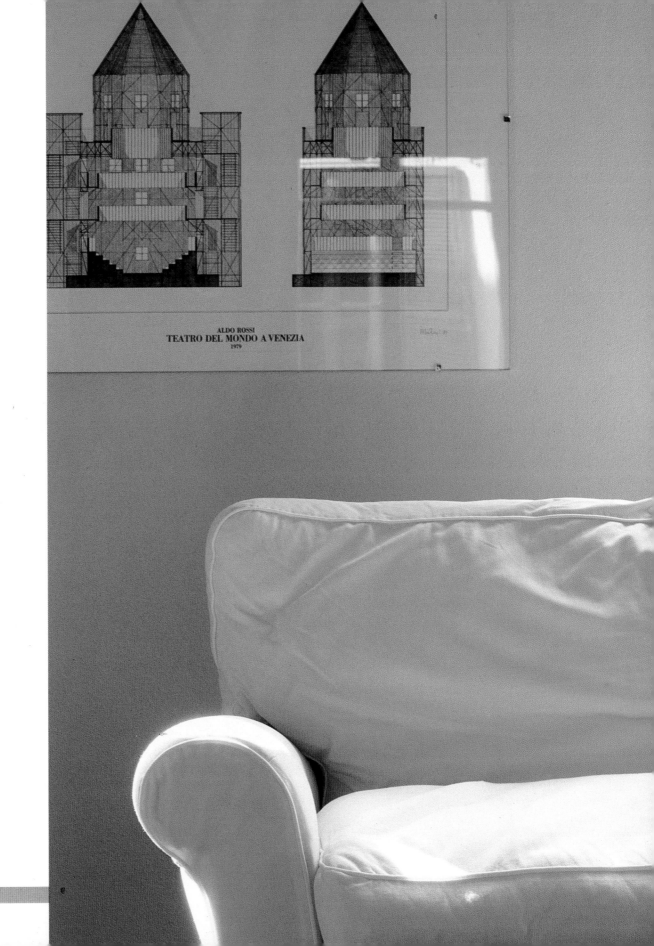

An architectural drawing by
Aldo Rossi is displayed above
one of the white sofas.

Clean geometric lines characterize the sparely furnished dining room on the first floor, below. The round table is marble; its elliptically shaped chairs are by Stephan Wewerka for Tecta. The lighting panels, used as a design element in other parts of the apartment, were designed by Piero Castiglioni. Another "Blackboard" rug by Eileen Gray covers the floor. The silkscreen is by Pistoletto. A metallic railing borders the second-level balcony of the apartment, left.

In one corner of the dining room, a classically inspired sculpture by Andrea Cascella was placed on a three-legged table designed by Marco Zanuso. The canvas is by Kounellis, and what appears to be an abstract wood sculpture lying on the floor is actually an extension for a modern Finnish table used for extra guests.

Seventeenth-century Italian paintings, left, are displayed in the small game area behind the main living room, below, for which Toni Cordero designed a linear black table and added inexpensive metal mesh chairs. The Genovese *capo d'opera* is also from the 17th century.

An intense red unites the various elements of a small, first-level bathroom near the entrance. It is the only room in the apartment that departs from the cool color scheme. The white marble bust is an early 20th-century work.

A harmony of gold and peach tones and the play of beautiful fabric add a special softness to the bedroom of the Milan apartment, right. The cotton lace bedspread is woven in a pattern popular in Lombardy during the 19th century. An antique Chinese textile embroidered with birds and flowers is fastened to the wall and ceiling as a headboard. The panel's reflection can be seen in the small mirror, far right, positioned above the cherrywood desk. The lamp is by Lalique.

mandelli/pinto

Once it had been an apartment that Mariuccia Mandelli Pinto described as "too modern—all plastic and chrome." "I longed for an environment that would be less up-to-the-minute," says Signora Pinto, who with her husband, Aldo, runs the Italian fashion house, Krizia. Now the penthouse in Milan's Porta Romana section resonates with personal spirit, redesigned to include and prominently display Signora Pinto's vases, lamps, and sculpture from the *floreale* and Art Deco periods.

Piero Pinto undertook the project for his brother and sister-in-law, beginning with the restructuring of the apartment: enlarging the living room, moving the dining and kitchen areas to the upper level near the ample terrace. The existing spiral staircase was replaced by Claude Lalanne's graceful *floreale*-styled "staircase-sculpture." Throughout the two levels is the subtle and extraordinary handiwork of Milanese artisans who painstakingly stenciled walls and mirrors and created bas-reliefs in the bathrooms.

"I always had a beige house," says Signora Pinto. "This time I searched for a warmer coloring." Walls were sponged with a glaze of gold, apricot, and peach watercolor, and the furnishings from the Sottsass-designed sofa to the divans upholstered in Fortuny fabric; the late 17th-century Japanese screens were chosen to harmonize with these rich tones. An animal motif runs throughout the apartment and everywhere one finds Signora Pinto's "zoo": serpent lamps, precious walking sticks with beautifully carved animal-head handles, embroidered silk panels of birds in flight, an oversized wood cricket, and porcelain and bronze animal figurines.

Ivory, ebony, silver, and wood walking sticks, each topped with a different animal head, and a dramatic Chinese canvas depicting two tigers greet visitors in the entrance foyer, left. The wood figures are Art Deco styled even though created by a contemporary English sculptor, Rod Dadley.

Signora Pinto collected Tiffany
lamps and vases from the Liberty and Art Deco periods for
over 25 years, but had no
appropriate place to display
them when the interior of her
apartment was 1960s modern
and most of the furniture either
glass or trimmed in chrome.
They are easily accommodated
in the newly designed interior
with its blend of early modern
styles. Among her favorite
pieces are opalescent calla lily
glass vases by Quezal, based
on a Tiffany model, above, and
the lily-of-the-valley Tiffany
lamp, right. The vases and lamp
are now located in the living
room.

The "staircase-sculpture," designed by Claude Lalanne, far right, interprets the *floreale* style in a modern way. The chairs, based on early 19th-century Russian models, are Italian reproductions made during the 1920s. Walls in the living room were sponged with watercolor to achieve the look of parchment.

On a small table in the living room, above, a Tiffany lamp is accompanied by a carefully arranged group of silver objects. A black-slate fireplace designed by Piero Pinto and black-lacquered console and tables accent the amber-tinged living room, right and above right, where sofas are covered in Fortuny fabric. Pinto chose the six-paneled 17th-century screen for its color and graphic depiction of a bridge. Ceramic animal figurines from the 18th century fill the round contemporary marble table.

Covering one bathroom wall is a delicate stucco bas-relief. The tree was sketched by Pinto and executed by local artisans.

The porcelain soap holder is *floreale* in design.

The *coiffeuse*, originally a fold-able writing desk for travel, and the stool are from the late 19th century. The vases are Lalique.

The large two-level terrace, below, has one of the most beautiful districts of Rome as its backdrop. A flowery panel, right, is part of the *floreale*-style screen at the entrance to director Lina Wertmüller's studio.

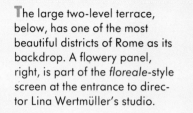

wertmüller/job

An apartment search in Rome can be as challenging as directing a movie. For Lina Wertmüller and her husband, Enrico Job, the noted sculptor and interior and set designer, it certainly seemed as time-consuming. But once they stepped onto the terrace of a turn-of-the-century apartment in downtown Rome and glimpsed the extraordinary view of the Piazza del Popolo with its majestic Egyptian obelisk, the pines of the Pincio hill, and the gardens of the Villa Borghese, they were instantly seduced.

The duplex apartment was renovated by Job to allow for relaxed and easy entertaining year-round, to accommodate his wife's need for a home-based studio, as well as to display their extensive collection of Tiffany lamps and their many pieces of furniture and sculpture from the *floreale,* or Italian Art Nouveau, period. "Both my wife and I are passionate about the *floreale* style," says Job. "We use it frequently in the design of our movie and stage sets."

Service rooms adjoin a small foyer on the entry level of the apartment. The walls of the stairway leading to the penthouse are covered with floor-to-ceiling mirrors and latticed oak paneling. To the right of the stairway is the master bedroom, to the left Lina Wertmüller's studio, separated from the living room by a multicolored *floreale*-style glass door. Both living and dining rooms look on to the terrace, which is used frequently for parties, and from early summer to early fall as Lina Wertmüller's warm-weather headquarters.

The living room on the penthouse level of the apartment, above, is located between the studio and dining area. Covering the ceiling is a large canvas once part of a theater set painted in the *floreale* style. Enrico Job was inspired by Dürer's engraving *Melencolia* to devise the wood-and-brass table, right, with numbers adding up to 34 in each direction. The digits three and four have symbolic meaning in Christianity and the Moslem religion respectively.

The foyer is home to two Sacchi Antropomorfici, anthromorphic sacks, created by Job, and a silkscreen by Michelangelo Pistoletti, above. The stairway and landing, right, were designed to convey the feeling of a gazebo.

Bronze figurines from the early 20th century and a Tiffany lamp are positioned on a living room table near one of Job's paintings, left. A *floreale*-style glass door leads to Lina Wertmüller's studio, above left. Positioned in front of the door and displayed prominently in the living room is one of the couple's most prized Tiffany lamps, above.

Early-morning sunlight fills Lina Wertmüller's tiny studio, usually a jungle of scripts and books. It has the same latticed paneling as that covering the walls of the stairway.

A beautiful mahogany bentwood bed by Thonet dominates the master bedroom. The bed covering is woven in a style popular in Italy during the 18th century.

The lace and linen bed pillows were delicately embroidered by local artisans.

Ernesto Basile, the most prominent architect of the Italian *floreale* period, designed the fireplace mantel located in the dining room.

The living room can be viewed from a porthole-shaped opening in the dining room wall, right. Above the opening is Nando Vigo's neon sculpture, dedicated to the signora of the house. The glass table in the dining room, far right, is the "Cugino" model by Enzo Mari for Driade.

fortunato

NEW SPACE IN A 16TH-CENTURY BUILDING

When a Milanese photographer asked architect Nanda Vigo to redesign his apartment, in a 16th-century building, one of the primary requirements was that the space be open, airy, and bright. Despite having been restructured over the centuries and having changed owners many times during the last decades, the apartment did have considerable plusses: ample room, well-preserved brick walls dating from the 17th century, and views of some of the most beautiful parks in Milan.

Nanda Vigo, an architect known for her striking interiors accented with glass, mirror, and neon sculpture, stripped the apartment of superfluous detailing and enlarged the space by transforming several terraces into glass-enclosed verandas. The minimal, carefully arranged furniture was designed by Vigo and other leading contemporary Italian designers. White laminate panels enclosing lighting fixtures were added directly beneath the ceiling. There are no doors in the public section of the apartment, with each area—entrance hall, living room, and dining room—flowing freely into one another.

"I wanted to bring the exterior inside," says Vigo, who insisted that the large windows and glass doors remain uncovered, allowing glimpses of greenery in spring and summer. Potted plants were used in each room and on the terrace, while hanging plants accent the living room, kitchen, and bath. A signature neon-sculpture, "visible poetry," decorates the circular opening between the living room and dining room.

Seventeenth-century brick walls, part of the original structure of the apartment and located in the entrance, below, and dining room, right, were restored during the apartment's renovation.

A large minimally furnished living room opens to sunny terraces that overlook the heart of Milan, above and right. Silk-covered daybeds by Antonia Astori for Driade serve as sofas. The laminate shelf was designed by Vigo. An Indian painting adds color to the room.

The bathroom was enlarged to include a veranda, which is now glass-enclosed. Appearing as a silhouette against the all-white room is a black cabinet, in the form of a female figure, which stores sponges and shells.

The kitchen, right, was considerably lengthened by extending one wall to contain a former balcony. In the center of the room is a table designed by Ettore Sottsass for Poltronova. Sliding doors are framed in aluminum. The simple, almost stark bedroom, below, includes an antique chaise and a bed designed by Vigo. Its patterned laminate headboard matches the surfaces of the wall-hung shelf. The wood chaise is from Kenya, the prints by Vasarély.

The *sala relax,* or family room, below, is used for informal entertaining. It leads to a roof garden affording spectacular views of downtown Milan. The chaise longues, covered in deep brown stretch fabric, and the globe lamp were designed by Gae Aulenti. The architectural model by Aldo Rossi, right, was executed as a design for Venice's Biennale. It stands on a stereo speaker at the entrance to the penthouse level.

carari

OPENING UP A PENTHOUSE DUPLEX

The penthouse duplex located in one of the oldest residential sections in Milan consisted of a banal assortment of small rooms that sliced up the apartment's ground floor. The layout was too constricting for the owners, a Milanese industrialist and his wife, and inadequate for their large collection of paintings, sculpture, and books, as well as their extensive music equipment. The architect, Gae Aulenti, eliminated the boxy rooms and reorganized the front of the apartment into a sweeping living/dining/office/library zone, and the back into a spacious arrangement of bedrooms, a bath, and a children's playroom.

Running along the first-level ceiling perimeter is an ingenious four-way steel track system which is used to suspend paintings, lighting fixtures, stereo speakers, and the thick canvas panels that cover the windows. Although a combination music center and bar divides the large public zone from the bedrooms and children's playroom, the two areas are united by background tones: beige carpeting runs throughout and all walls are painted a softly reflective white lacquer. The living room, simply furnished with contemporary and early 20th-century modern Italian pieces, is sectioned from the dining room by bookshelves. Designed to be several feet short of the ceiling, the shelves create private work space without interfering with the visual flow of the expansive entertainment zone.

On the penthouse level, Aulenti created a terraced belvedere, a complete *sala relax* for movie and television viewing, exercising, and casual entertaining. She also designed some of the apartment's furniture: the sleek chaise longues, the stools in the *sala relax,* the dining room table, the bookcases, and many of the lamps on the first floor.

The long console, right, covered with carpeting, was designed by Aulenti as a combination bar and music center— storing records, cassettes, tape recorder, and stereo turntable. It is located near the entrance to the apartment. A painting by David Hockney and lighting fixtures are suspended from a ceiling track system, also by Aulenti.

A chair from the early 1900s by Carlo Bugatti stands between a Francis Bacon painting and a Henry Moore sculpture in the living room, right. The large sculpture, fully visible above, was positioned at the entrance to the living room for maximum impact. Italian cashmere covers the contemporary sofas. The white marble table was designed by Aulenti.

Bookshelves, several feet short
of the ceiling, create a secluded
work area and library on the
apartment's first level. The Italian brierwood table is from the
1930s. The small wood chair in
the background, covered with
white leather, is by Bugatti.
Resting on top of the bookcases
are metal sculptures by Fausto
Melotti and an assortment of
Murano, Loetz, Gallé, and
Schneider vases.

The small dining room, above, is located directly behind the office. The tapestry, called "The World," is by the contemporary Italian artist Alighiero Boetti. The black marble table and white marble étagère were designed by Aulenti. An arrangement of black and red blown-glass vases from Murano is displayed in the center of the table, right. The painting is by Magritte.

As strong as the Italian love for the past is their fascination with the daring, the new. In the last several years, certain Milan-based furniture collectives as well as the exhibition work of architects such as Alessandro Mendini, Ettore Sottsass, and Giò Ponti have sought to challenge even the most modern concepts of design with the creation of highly provocative, often allegorical, sometimes shocking, yet never boring pieces of furniture. Their goal is to reinvent a language of signs and imagery and to force a reevaluation of the way furniture is perceived and used by experimenting with new materials, contrasting patterns and textures, and unusual shapes. Often lacking in familiar elements or references, these radical design works are rarely used exclusively in one environment, but their message and appearance are so distinctive that the impact on home furnishings has been felt worldwide.

The cube-shaped house, below and right, which is located near Monza, a Milan suburb, is divided into two equal-sized duplex apartments by a thick cement wall. The two cylinders incorporate interior staircases. Stripes of varying widths were painted on the house's exterior walls for graphic impact. Sliding panels cover large windows on both levels.

arosio

I wanted a blend of art, sculpture, and architecture," says architect Lino Arosio, who with Alberto Salvati and Ambrogio Tresoldi conceived of the unconventional design of this two-story villa located in a suburb of Milan. The layout is based on geometric shapes: a cube with two cylinders on the facade split precisely in half by a thick cement wall. On each side there's an identical duplex apartment, one for Signor Arosio, the other for his brother.

Rather than paint the house brick, mustard, or terra-cotta, traditional hues for Italian houses and apartment buildings, Arosio decided to cover the cylinders and the rectangular panels on the exterior of the villa with yellow, orange-red, and blue stripes of varying widths. The colors Arosio describes as "technical" were chosen to refer to hydraulic parts—yellow for gas, orange-red for hot water, and blue for cold water. The panels, which align vertically along the edge of each exterior wall, slide to open and close windows on both levels.

More subdued tones were selected for the interior: gray for walls, pink for lacquer-finished doors and cabinets, white for the kitchen and fireplace laminate. Floors are covered in deep gray porfido stone, which is set in a large mosaiclike pattern, also found on the exterior and interior steps of the villa and along the driveway.

Living room, dining room, and kitchen are arranged in a U-shaped layout on the main floor of Lino Arosio's apartment. The second level has only the master bedroom, bath, and a landing, all connected by a small walkway and bordered by a cement balcony. The apartment's furnishings were designed to be practical and space-saving: a fireplace mantel doubles as a storage unit, a dining table folds neatly into a sleek cabinet. The spareness also dramatizes the collection of artwork and sculpture.

Soft tones of gray, pink, white, and pastel green appear throughout the interior. A conversation area was created in the living room with an arrangement of Cassina AEO chairs, which were introduced in Italy during the early 1970s. Stone pavement is used for all indoor flooring and for the steps and driveway outdoors. Armando Marocco's sculpture alludes to the arrows of Achilles. Beneath the arrows Marocco assembled a collection of real and plastic rocks to symbolize natural and artificial elements in art and life.

Papier-mâché columns, right, symbols of Stonehenge, are located in the entrance to the dining room. The triangular table was designed by Lino Arosio; the American wall sculpture above depicts an enormous match.

The dining table, below, folds into the pink laminate cabinet. The colorful grid sculpture, produced by the Italian company Jabik, was chosen by Arosio as the centerpiece for its transparency and geometric form.

A narrow balcony, above, borders the small walkway that links the master bedroom, bath, and landing. The Marocco arrow sculpture, right, forms an arc over the balcony and descends into the living room.

Vertical blinds create striped patterns of light in the soft-toned master bedroom. The acrylic painting above the bed is by Giuliano Barbanti, an Italian abstract artist. The metal bar is part of a clothing stand.

Mock room dividers by Gaetano Pesce, a prominent Italian architect and sculptor, hold a selection of books and small stick sculpture by Armando Marocco on the shelves. Ugo Nespolo, an Italian neofigurative artist, designed the oversized fruit. The soup can, called "Omaggio a Warhol" (Homage to Warhol), is actually a small stool and is produced by Simon International.

The dining table, right, is covered in a reflective laminate that allows a variety of decorative objects to be affixed to its surface and legs. A black plaque by a contemporary artist, etched with calligraphy, a yellow wolf's-head sculpture, and the reflection of bright red anthurium create an enigmatic still life. The table and the lacquered chairs, far right, are Mendini designs for Studio Alchimia.

beretta

When interiors photographer Ambrogio Beretta felt it was time to revitalize his apartment in an old section of Milan, he turned to a colleague for help. Architect Alessandro Mendini, the editorial director of *Domus* and the guiding spirit behind Studio Alchimia, a furniture collective in the vanguard of Italian design, accepted the project on one condition—that there would be no design limitations. Beretta, who had long admired Mendini's work, willingly gave him free reign, and promptly turned over all his furnishings to storage. "I decided my apartment should reflect a synthesis of new ideas rather than be a collection of memories," says Beretta.

Mendini filled the apartment with some of the most experimental furniture he'd ever designed. Although traditionally functional pieces were used—a sofa in the living room, a table and chairs in the dining room, a bed and night table in the bedroom—they are widely divergent in form and color from the furniture one might expect to see. Mendini's inspiration came from a variety of sources, including a Shakespearean tragedy, and postwar industrial design, but most often from the 20th century's earliest avant-garde movements—Cubism, Futurism, Dadaism. Mendini calls his design approach "neomodern," to distinguish it from postmodernism, which draws on a classical past.

About the time the new interior was completed, an experimental theater group known to both Mendini and Beretta was looking for an unusual setting for their play *Un Milione di Domani* ("A Million Tomorrows"). Beretta suggested his apartment, which became the theater for the psychological drama, with actors and spectators moving throughout the rooms during each performance. "An actor can perform in an apartment as easily as a man can live in a theatrical setting," says Mendini, who likened the Beretta apartment to an avant-garde stage set. After the last performance of the play, which ran for 20 nights, Beretta moved in to find the environment "ideal." He says, "I'm happier with this interior, which I find inspiring for developing new visual concepts."

Multicolored "island-puzzles," Alessandro Mendini's interpretations of a wall tapestry and floor runner, are made in leather. He also designed the violet sofa, called "Sabrina," for Driade, along the lines of the chairs created by the prominent Italian architect Giò Ponti in the late 1950s. Books are arranged casually on the floor.

The corridor, left, has a swirling lighting fixture, called "Urbulante," which in the experimental play performed in the apartment symbolized a man's flight over a city.

The "Modulando," located in the kitchen, expands the traditional notion of a commode, right. Mendini designed it with a humorous touch, varying the forms of its bases and appliqués. The two feet supporting the piece loosely depict a flag and an amoeba.

The small bedroom, above and above right, is dominated by the "bed of flowers," one of six originally designed by Mendini for the Verona exhibit Casa per Giulietta (Juliet's House). The night table, seemingly suspended in midair by an almost invisible set of string supports, has just enough room for a small television set and vase.

Practical considerations, such
as closet space, were not over-
looked in designing the interior
furnishings for the apartment.
Called an *armadio molle,* or
soft armoire, the wardrobe,
right, is a one-of-a-kind piece.
The white mask, a theatrical
reference, is by Mendini.

Televisions and audio-video equipment rest on marbleized wood columns, forming what members of the Studio Metamorfosi describe as "A Monument to 'Struttura Assente,'" as all of the components can be programmed to function automatically without human intervention. The entrance to the studio, right, places a contemporary cultural icon, a TV set, on a faux-marbre pedestal.

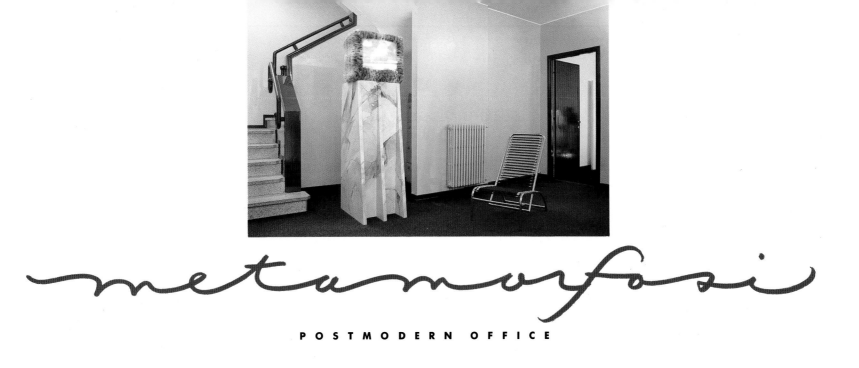

metamorfosi

The seven partners of the Studio Metamorfosi, a Milan-based music and fashion video-cassette production company, wanted their one-room office space to symbolize the nature of their work, which embraces the avant-garde and is as experimental as the company name suggests. The architects for the project were Bruno Gregori and Yumiko Kobayashi, both of Studio Alchimia.

The central element in the work/reception room is a five-meter-long black metal table designed by Alessandro Mendini. Its purpose originally was quite simple and traditional—to serve as a conference table. It was gradually "metamorphosized," as Mendini says, "to keep pace with the Studio's needs." The legs of the table were ingeniously and invisibly wired to allow electric current to reach the television set and push-button phones, which were built into the table surface, as well as lighting fixtures, computers, and a coffee machine, which are frequently used by studio members.

Four video-television sets are arranged for client viewing on faux-marbre wood pedestals. Other postmodern elements include a Studio Alchimia-designed white laminate aqueduct, which serves as sculpture and room divider. A wood column with faux-marbre painted finish displays a leopard-skin-covered television set at the entrance to the studio. Sculpture by Mendini and the video artist Lia Bottanelli further dramatizes the unusual office, which its designers characterize as a testimony to the theory of "Struttura Assente"—that is, space that could function effectively with or without man's presence.

The long black metal conference table runs almost the entire length of the studio. Windows are covered with simple cotton panels, and floors with charcoal industrial carpeting.

The white metal table lamp, which has its equivalent in a floor version in another part of the studio, was designed by Alessandro Mendini for Alchimia. The wall art was made in metal, wood, and printed fabric by the Italian artist Lia Botanelli. None of the office chairs placed around the conference table are the same, as each member of the studio selected a different piece for personal use.

The conference table, its legs electrically wired, has a built-in TV and phone. In the background are two Mendini sculptures, the mirrored "Arredo Vestitivo" or "furniture to wear" (so described as a person may actually experience the piece by putting it on, which Mendini felt would symbolize the infinite possibilities of architecture and fashion) and the white laminate aqueduct, serving as both sculpture and at times as a room divider.

The asymmetrical chair called "Bel Air," right, was designed by Peter Shire and is part of the Memphis collection. The clock-sculpture resting atop the yellow lacquered desk is the work of English artist Daniel Weil. Near the entrance to the studio, far right, a Memphis sofa called "Lido" and an abstract painting by Sandro Martini provide a colorful contrast to the large striped column created by the Austrian designer Jorrit Tornquist.

melzi

ARTFUL WORK SPACE

When Giuseppe Melzi, a young lawyer with an expanding collection of conceptual and abstract art, rented an office in the most central district in Milan within view of the 14th-century Duomo, he asked the architectural team of Salvati and Tresoldi to develop a space that could efficiently serve his business needs, yet not resemble a traditional office. "Since I spend most of my day here and often sleep over too, I consider this my true home," says Melzi who also maintains a residence in Milan. "I wanted this environment to be easy to live and work in, to be colorful and stimulating."

One enters the office through a long corridor accented with Memphis furniture and two enormous canvas panels, the work of a young Italian artist, Giorgio Griffa. A sweep of Armando Marocco arrows links the corridor with the heart of the studio, an abstract arrangement of walls, one angular and one curved. These walls were designed to help define the vast open office space and serve as a backdrop for the Marocco sculpture, a series of "Achilles" arrows, the last one piercing the angled wall, and two bronze medallions, illuminated and displayed on the inner side of the curved structure. Directly adjacent to these central walls are two open work spaces.

All the bookcases and desks were designed by Salvati and Tresoldi; the chairs, sofas, lamps, and clocks are from the Memphis collection or the work of young European artists. Almost all the furniture is brightly colored. "The basic lines of the pieces, the purity of the colors, I find soothing in a working atmosphere," says Melzi. "My clients relax more easily, too, without the imagery of the standard office surrounding them."

Giorgio Griffa's canvas panels cover two of the studio walls, below. Both sofas, the vibrant "Lido" and marble "Agra," were designed by Michele de Lucchi for Memphis. Slate pavement runs throughout the studio.

Inspired by the graphic painting of Piet Mondrian, bookcases in the various studio offices are painted in bright contrasting colors, above. The architectural team of Salvati and Tresoldi designed them as well as the office desks. George James Sowden's "Palace" chairs for Memphis provide other rich accents. Flanking one wall is Peter Shire's "Hollywood" table, also part of the Memphis collection.

A curved wall was constructed in the center of the studio and serves as a counterpoint to the furniture and art's rigorous lines. A bronze allegorical sculpture by Armando Marocco, part of a pair called "Iside" and "Osiride," is illuminated on the inside of the wall. Another Marocco sculpture intersects the outside triangular wall. Alluding to Achilles arrows, Marocco titled it "Achilles Could Not Escape His Fate."

Even the terrace of Karl Lagerfeld's 21st-floor Monte Carlo apartment includes Memphis pieces. The black marble and glass table was designed by Ettore Sottsass, the metal and wood chairs, below and right, by Michele de Lucchi. An antique statue contrasts with the avant-garde pieces. The rug, "Turkish Nude," by Eileen Gray, is from the 1920s.

lagerfeld

The 18th-century Paris apartment and town house, the chateau in Brittany, and the Rome *pied-à-terre* were filled with exquisite antiques, but fashion designer Karl Lagerfeld's high-rise apartment in Monte Carlo demanded a totally new approach. Assisted by French decorator Andrée Putman, Lagerfeld selected furniture from the first two Memphis collections to fill the 1,200-square-foot residence he describes as an "apartment without a past."

With the exception of the entrance area's Helmut Newton photographs, the gray-painted walls were left undecorated to provide a soothing backdrop for the clash of Memphis pieces. The works of this Italian-based international design collective can be characterized—if at all—by their unexpected blending of materials, patterns, surfaces, and textures, their intentional failure to coordinate, and their ability to be used in whatever context the owner sees fit to use them.

The large living room faces on to the terrace and is loosely organized into two sections, one for receiving guests and friends, the other for dining. A striped boxing ring, designed by Masanori Umeda, serves as a conversation zone, surrounded by Sottsass-designed bookcases and lighting fixtures. A white laminate table and set of chairs, and a sideboard displaying tea sets and vases are the only furnishings in the dining section. Rubber flooring runs through all the rooms. Originally black, the salty sea air has turned it a deep gray.

Lagerfeld, the highly innovative couturier who designs under his own name, as well as for Chanel and as a contributing designer to Fendi, uses his Monte Carlo home as a work retreat rather than as a vacation spot. One of the first all-Memphis environments in the world, the apartment is a creative inspiration to its owner, appealing to his fondness for the iconoclastic and satisfying his need for change.

Dominating the living room is Masanori Umeda's striped boxing ring, the Memphis interpretation of a conversation pit. The multicolored, multiangled *libreria* is a Sottsass design.

The entrance foyer, above, painted a deep gray like the living room, has a brightly colored "Dublin" sofa by Marco Zanuso, a "Tree-tops" lamp by Sottsass, and a spacious wardrobe, left, created by the Memphis designer Matteo Thun. The large framed photographs are by Helmut Newton; they appeared in the book *Big Nudes*, for which Lagerfeld wrote the introduction.

Vases, tea sets, and lighting fixtures arranged in the living room echo the distinctive contours of the apartment's Memphis furniture. Designed to hold a single flower each, the porcelain vases, left, by Matteo Thun, are called "Volga" and "Danubio." Sotsass created the silver teapot, above, and the halogen lamp called "Quisisana," right.

An informal dining area, below, was created in one section of the living room. The "Riviera" chairs were designed by de Lucchi. They are made of plastic laminate and have back and seat cushions covered in cotton chintz. The metal and laminate sideboard is by Sottsass: Each shelf's metal supports vary in color and shape. The space capsule-like object, right, on a sideboard shelf, is actually a teapot.

Thun created most of the teapots on the sideboard, above, especially for Lagerfeld.

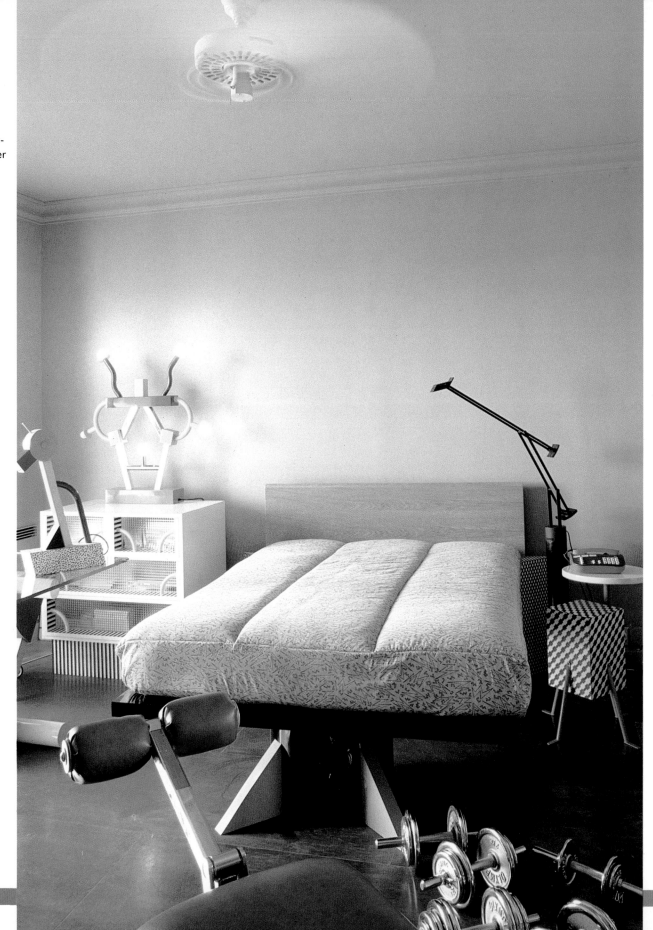

Richard Sapper's Tizio lamp, and lighting fixtures designed by Sottsass flank Lagerfeld's bed. The fabric for the bed covering is by Nathalie du Pasquier for Memphis.

The range of Italian furniture and products in the United States has increased enormously in the past ten years. Our directory attempts to include as many listings as possible for anyone interested in Italian antiques, tiles, fabrics, lighting fixtures, and modern and avant-garde furniture. Considering that many Americans travel to Italy, we have also included a short listing of furniture and lighting sources in Milan, Florence, and Rome favored by our Italian collaborators.

Our sources include retail (R), wholesale (W) ("to the trade," or to decorators only), and mail order (MO) outlets, and a small listing of highly skilled artists specializing in trompe l'oeil and other decorative effects, who are willing to work anywhere in the United States. The addresses of primary locations for antiques shops and retail and wholesale outlets, as well as the locations of branch stores and offices are provided. If no listing in your area is offered, you will be able to find the address and phone number of the store nearest you by getting in touch with the main office. Addresses, phone numbers, and descriptions are up to date as we go to press.

FOR FURNITURE AND OBJECTS

TRADITIONAL

Didier Aaron, Inc.
32 East 67th St.
New York, NY 10021
212-988-5248

Didier Aaron Ltd.
9002 Melrose Ave.
Los Angeles, CA 90069
213-273-3037
Eighteenth- and 19th-century Italian antiques, paintings, and decorative accessories; Empire furniture. (R) (W)

Ace Galleries
91 University Pl.
New York, NY 10003
212-260-2720
Eighteenth- and 19th-century Italian antiques and country furniture; armoires. (W)

Ariadne Galleries
970 Madison Ave.
New York, NY 10021
212-772-3388
Greek and Roman antiquities, ancient art, coins, Byzantine art. (R) (W)

Mid-18th-century frescoed headboard. Renzo Olivieri

Artisan Antiques
989 Second Ave.
New York, NY 10022
212-751-5214
Nineteenth-century Italian antiques and decorative accessories; mirrors, mosaics, bronzes. (R) (W)

David Barett Circa Ltd.
979 Third Ave., Rm. 1105
New York, NY 10022
212-688-0950
Nineteenth-century Italian antiques. (R) (W)

Berges
1015 Madison Ave.
New York, NY 10021
212-879-2846
Seventeenth and 18th-century Italian furniture.

Michael Capo Antiques
831 Broadway
New York, NY 10003
212-982-9710
Seventeenth-, 18th- and 19th-century furniture. Many Northern Italian and Venetian pieces. (W)

Christie's New York
502 Park Ave.
New York, NY 10022
212-546-1150 (European furniture department)
212-546-1000 (for information about auctions and sales)

21-24 44th Ave.
Long Island City, NY 11101
718-784-1480 (For sales catalogues, auction news, newsletter, the *Christie's*

International Magazine.)
Sixteenth- to 19th-century Italian antiques and decorative accessories.

East and Orient Company
2901 North Henderson Ave.
Dallas, TX 75206
214-826-1191
Seventeenth- to 19th-century Italian antiques and decorative accessories. (R) (W)

Gallery 63 Antiques
1050 Second Ave.
New York, NY 10022
212-751-0367
Eighteenth- and 19th-century Italian antiques; carved furniture, marble sculpture, and decorative accessories. (R) (W)

Otto Gerdau Import and Export Co.
82 Wall St.
New York, NY 10005
212-709-9600
Pickle pine reproductions of Italian Louis XV- and XVI-style chairs. (W)

Richard Himmel Design Pavilion
219 West Erie St.
Chicago, IL 60610
312-266-0002

Eighteenth-century Italian furniture. (R) (W)

Imports for the Trade, Inc.
26 N.E. 27th St.
Miami, FL 33137
305-573-1330
Reproductions of a range of Italian period furniture. (W)

Maison des Arts
1015 Madison Ave.
New York, NY 10021
212-517-7733
Eighteenth-century Italian furniture and decorative accessories. (R) (W)

Late-18th-century demilune. Renzo Olivieri

Malmaison, Inc.
29 East 10th St.
New York, NY 10003
212-473-0373
Late-18th- and early-
19th-century Italian
neoclassical painted and
fruitwood antiques. (R) (W)

————

Manhattan Art and
Antiques Center
1050 Second Ave.
New York, NY 10022
212-355-4400
Eighteenth- and 19th-
century Italian antiques
and rugs. (R) (W)

————

Martin of London: Fine
Replicas and Antiques
8401 Melrose Pl.

Los Angeles, CA 90069
213-653-1566
Seventeenth-, 18th-, and
19th-century Italian
furniture; bronzes. (W)

————

Newel Art Galleries
425 East 53rd St.
New York, NY 10022
212-758-1970
Eighteenth- and 19th-
century Italian antiques.
(W)

————

Renzo Olivieri
306 East 61st St.
New York, NY 10021
212-355-0413 or
212-838-7281
Eighteenth- and 19th-

century Italian antiques
and decorative
accessories. (R)

————

Frank Pellitteri, Inc.
201 East 56th St.
New York, NY 10022
212-486-0545
Seventeenth-, 18th-, and
19th-century Italian
antiques. (W)

————

Royal Athena Galleries
153 East 57th St.
New York, NY 10022
212-355-2034
Roman, Byzantine
sculpture; marble and
bronze vases. (R) (W)

————

Safani Gallery
960 Madison Ave.
New York, NY 10021
212-570-6360
Bronzes and sculpture
from the early Roman
period to the second and
third centuries A.D. (R) (W)

————

Sotheby Parke Bernet, Inc.
1334 York Ave. at 72nd St.
New York, NY 10021
212-606-7000
(For 24-hour auction and
exhibition information
call 212-606-7245.)

Italian furniture and
decorative works of art,
paintings, and drawings
from the late Renaissance
to the 19th century.

————

Gabriel Victor Custom
Furniture Collections
9046 Culver Blvd.
Culver City, CA 90230
213-837-8775
Reproductions of a wide
range of Italian antiques;
custom-made furniture.
(R) (W)

————

ANTIQUARI IN ITALY

————

Antonacci
Via del Babuino 146
Roma
06/6781595
Late-19th-century Italian
antiques and decorative
objects. (R)

————

Bellini
Lungarno Soderini 5
Roma
055/214031
Fifteenth- and 16th-
century Tuscan antiques
and decorative objects. (R)

————

Christie's Milano
(representative office)
Via Borgogna 9
20122 Milano
02/794712

Christie's Roma
Piazza Navona 114
00186 Roma
06/6564032
Italian antiques from the 16th to 19th centuries. Auctions only in Rome.

Di Castro
Via del Babuino 71
Roma
06/6794900
Late 17th- and early-18th-century baroque antiques. **(R)**

Luzzetti
Borgo San Jacopo 28/A
Firenze
055/211232
Antiques from central Italy, generally from the 15th and 16th centuries. **(R)**

Orsi
Via Bagutta 14
Milano
02/702214
Paintings, sculpture, 18th-century decorative objects from Lombardy and the Veneto; Renaissance bronzes. **(R)**

Sotheby Parke Bernet Italia
Palazzo Capponi
Via Gino Capponi 26
50121 Firenze
055/571410

Via Montenapoleone 3
20121 Milano
02/783907

Palazzo Taverna
Via di Monte Giordano 26
00186 Roma

06/6561670 and 06/6547400
Sixteenth- to 19th-century Italian antiques and decorative accessories.

Alberto Subert
Via Spiga 22
Milano
02/799594
Antiques and decorative objects; paintings from the 17th and 18th centuries. **(R)**

Giltwood and gesso-painted mirror, mid-18th century. Auctioned at Christie's

Trois
Via XXII Marzo 2251
Venezia
041/22905
Eighteenth-century Italian antiques. **(R)**

Didier Aaron, Inc.
37 East 67th St.
New York, NY 10021
212-988-5248

Didier Aaron Ltd.
9002 Melrose Ave.
Los Angeles, CA 90069
213-273-3037
Ruhlmann and Art Deco furniture. **(R) (W)**

Arango
7519 Dadeland Mall
Miami, FL 33156
305-661-4229

The Galleria
2384 East Sunrise Blvd.
Ft. Lauderdale, FL 33304
305-563-6688
Contemporary Italian furnishings; accessories by Danese, Artemide, Castelli, Arnolfo di Cambio, Alessi. **(R)**

Architectural Antiques Exchange
709-15 North Second St.

Philadelphia, PA 19123
215-922-3669
Art Nouveau and Art Deco furniture; Thonet chairs; marble statues.
(R) (W)

Doré bronze, marble, and enamel dancer by Chiparus. Gallery 63

Artemide, Inc.
150 East 58th St.
New York, NY 10155
212-980-0710

851 Merchandise Mart
Chicago, IL 60654
312-644-0510

266 Pacific Design Center
8687 Melrose Ave.
Los Angeles, CA 90069
213-659-1708
Molded glass fiber
reinforced polyester
furniture; dining and
cocktail tables, umbrella
and coat stands; wall
mirrors. (W)

Artisan Antiques, Inc./
Art Deco
999 Second Ave.
New York, NY 10022
212-750-8892
Art Deco furniture,
statues, bronzes, lighting
fixtures. (R) (W)

Atelier International Ltd.
595 Madison Ave.
New York, NY 10022
212-644-0400

9-100 Merchandise Mart
Chicago, IL 60654
312-329-0360

608 World Trade Center

Marcuso table by Marco
Zanuso. I.C.F.

Dallas, TX 75258
214-653-1161

8687 Melrose Ave.
Los Angeles, CA 90069
213-659-9402

300 D St., S.W.
Washington, DC 20024
202-484-1287
Other showrooms in
Branford, Conn.; Boston,
Mass.; Coral Gables,
Fla.; Denver, Colo.;
Seattle, Wash.; call the
New York office.
Furniture from the Italian
companies Acerbis,
Cassina, Ibis, Marcatre;
designs by Mario Bellini,
Vico Magistretti, Afra
and Tobia Scarpa, Giotto
Stoppino; reproductions
of modern classics by Le
Corbusier, Charles
Rennie Mackintosh,
Garrit Rietveld. (W)

Axiom Designs
110 Greene St.
New York, NY 10012
212-219-2212

200 Kanasas St. #25
San Francisco, CA 94103
415-864-6688
Contemporary Italian
sofas and chairs;
upholstered modular
furniture. (W)

Beylerian Ltd.
305 East 63rd St., 15th fl.
New York, NY 10021
212-755-6300

1198 Merchandise Mart
Chicago, IL 60654
312-670-2220
Contemporary Italian
chairs, tables, desks,
storage systems, and
accessories in wood,
leather, metal; furniture
designed by Cini Boeri,

Achille and Pier Giacomo
Castiglioni, Eileen Gray.
(R) (W)

Casa Bella
979 Third Ave.
New York, NY 10022
212-688-2020

3750 Biscayne Blvd.
Miami, FL 33137
305-573-0800
For additional
showrooms in Chicago,
Ill.; Dallas and Houston,
Tex.; and Los Angeles,
Cal., call Casa Bella in
Miami, Fla.
Contemporary Italian
furniture and accessories
by Casa Bella designers.
(W)

Castelli Furniture, Inc.
950 Third Ave.
New York, NY 10022
212-751-2050

1150 Merchandise Mart
Chicago, IL 60654
312-828-0200
Plia chairs. (W)

Christie's New York
502 Park Ave.
New York, NY 10022
212-546-1086 (modern
furniture department)
212-546-1000 (for
information about
auctions and sales).
Mid-19th-century to
present-day furniture and
decorative arts.

City
312 West Institute Pl.
Chicago, IL 60610
312-664-9581
Seccosi bookcases, carts;
Moltini anodized
aluminum stacking
chairs; contemporary
furniture from Theema
and Magis. (R) (MO)

Flavio Poli vases, 1958. Fifty-
50, New York

EEVA-INKERI

Armless chair and armchair by Gae Aulenti. Knoll International

Carlo Mollino side chair, 1948. Fifty-50, New York

MICHAEL NORGART

Contemporary Galleries, Inc.
221 West Fourth St.
Cincinnati, OH 45202
513-621-3113
Other stores in
Charleston, W. Va.;
Dayton, Ohio; Lexington
and Louisville, Ky.
Kartell plastic furniture,
EMU outdoor furniture. (R)

———

Crate and Barrel
190 Northfield Rd.
Northfield, IL 60093
312-446-9300
Other stores in Boston
and Cambridge, Mass.;
Chicago, Ill.; Dallas, Tex.
Outdoor furniture and
umbrellas. (R)

———

Conran's
160 East 54th St.
New York, NY 10022
212-371-0998

145 Huguenot St.
New Rochelle, NY 10801
(for catalogue)

Other stores in
Hackensack, N.J.;
King of Prussia, Pa.;
Manhasset, N.Y.;
Washington, D.C.;
White Plains, N.Y.
Contemporary,
moderately priced Italian
furniture and decorative
accessories. (R) (MO)

Current
815 East Thomas
Seattle, WA 98102
206-325-2995
Contemporary Italian
chairs, tables, cabinets,
upholstered furniture;
reproductions of modern
classic furniture by Le
Corbusier, Mies van der
Rohe, Marcel Breuer;
decorative accessories by
Rexite, SIAT, Sicart, ICM,
NAVA. (R) (W)

———

Designers Furniture
Center International

150 East 58th St.
New York, NY 10155
212-755-5611

979 Third Ave.
New York, NY 10022
212-755-5611
Contemporary Italian
tables, chairs, and buffets
in lacquer and marble
and natural wood. (W)

———

Domus
1214 Perimeter Mall
4400 Ashford-Dunwoody
Rd.
Atlanta, GA 30346
404-396-1064
Modern Italian furniture
and decorative
accessories. (R) (MO)

———

East and Orient Co.
2901 North Henderson
Ave.
Dallas, TX 75206
214-826-1191
Art Nouveau and Art
Deco furniture; pieces by

Eileen Gray, Joseph
Hoffmann, Emile-Jacques
Ruhlmann, Michael
Thonet. (R) (W)

———

Ello Furniture Manuf. Co.
1034 Elm St.
Rockford, IL 61101
815-964-8601
Contemporary Italian
tables, chairs, bedroom
furniture; travertine and
marble accessories; high-
gloss lacquer chairs and
case goods. (W)

EMU/USA, Inc.
1129 Magnolia Ave.
Larkspur, CA 94939
415-461-2633

135 Fort Lee Rd.
P.O. Box 206
Leonia, NJ 07605
201-585-9420
Plastic-coated steel
outdoor furniture from
EMU Spa. (W)

———

Fabrications
146 East 56th St.
New York, NY 10022

CAB armchair by Mario Bellini. Atelier International. La Loggia table by Mario Bellini. Cassina, Italy

MICHAEL NORGART

212-371-3370
Contemporary Italian
foldable furniture. (R) (W)

Fifty-50
793 Broadway
New York, NY 10003
212-777-3208
Giò Ponti coffee tables
and dining chairs; chairs
by Marco Zanuso for
Arflex, Noguchi-designed
furniture. Postwar Italian
art glass, Venini glass
and Italian ceramics. (R)

Sam Flax
55 East 55th St.
New York, NY 10022
212-620-3000
Phone orders: 800-221-
9818 (outside New York
State), 800-522-7111 (in
New York State). Other
stores in Atlanta, Ga.;
Tampa, Fla.; Woburn,
Mass.
Bieffe drafting tables,
chairs, and storage units.
(R) (W) (MO)

Furniture of the Twentieth
Century
227 West 17th St.
New York, NY 10011
212-929-6023
Modern furniture by
Bieffeplast, Longoni,
Terragni, Zanotta. (W)

Gallery 63 Antiques
1050 Second Ave.
New York, NY 10022
212-751-0367
Art Nouveau and Art
Deco sculpture; works by
Chiparus, Zach, Chalon,
Preiss, Phillipe, Gallè
glass. (R) (W)

Otto Gerdau Co.
Import and Export
82 Wall St.
New York, NY 10005
212-709-9600
Contemporary lacquer
chairs; marble cocktail
and dining tables. (W)

Gia International Design
430 East 59th St.
New York, NY 10022
212-753-4255
Showrooms in Chicago,
Ill.; Dallas, Tex.;
Hacienda Heights and
Los Angeles, Cal.
Contemporary Italian
upholstered and wood
furniture. (W)

Richard Himmel Design
Pavilion
219 West Erie St.
Chicago, IL 60610
312-266-0002
European Art Nouveau
and Art Deco, Ruhlmann
pieces. (R) (W)

ALDO BALLO

**Cumano table by Achille Cas-
tiglioni. Zanotta, Italy**

Interna Designs Ltd.
Merchandise Mart
Space 6-168
Chicago, IL 60654
312-467-6076
Cappellini, Driade,
Poltrona Frau, Zanotta
Furniture, Kilm Carpets
by Renata Bonfonti. (W)

International Contract
Furnishings, Inc.
305 East 63rd St.
New York, NY 10021
212-750-0900

945 Merchandise Mart
Chicago, IL 60654
312-222-0160

**Drop-front secretary by Giò
Ponti, screen design by Piero
Fornasetti. Fifty-50**

8687 Melrose Ave.
Los Angeles, CA 90069
213-659-1387

818 25th St.
Denver, CO 80205
303-296-9118

1365 Peachtree St.
Atlanta, GA 30309
404-876-6367

3233 Weslayan
Houston, TX 77027
713-840-7924

3311 M Street NW
Washington, DC 20007
202-298-7941
Contemporary Italian and
international furniture;
the Anfibio sofa, Basilio
dining table by Marco
Zanuso, Berillo bar stool
by Joe Colombo, De Pas,
D'Urbino and Lomazzi
sectional seating, Elle
chairs, Marcuso table by
Marco Zanuso,
Mezzadro tractor seat by
Achille and Pier Giacomo
Castiglioni, OMK tables
and chairs, Gabriele
Mucchi chair and
ottoman, Primate

kneeling stool by Achille
Castiglioni, Sacco
beanbag, Spaghetti
chairs and table (W)

———

Kartell/USA
225 Fifth Ave.
New York, NY 10010
212-889-9111

Box 1000
Liberty Highway
Easley, SC 29640
1-800-845-2517
High-tech plastic
furniture and decorative
accessories. (W)

———

Knoll International
655 Madison Ave.
New York, NY 10021
212-826-2400

105 Wooster St.
New York, NY 10012
212-219-6500
Contemporary Italian and
international furniture;
furniture designed by

Gae Aulenti, Cini Boeri,
Tobia Scarpa, Massimo
and Lella Vignelli;
modern classics by
Breuer, Florence Knoll,
Mies van der Rohe,
Eero Saarinen. (W)

———

Loewenstein, Inc.
3260 S.W. 11th Ave.
P.O. Box 22029
Fort Lauderdale, FL
33335
305-525-8453
Modern seating, stacking
steel chairs and stools,
upholstered chairs,
dining tables. (W)

———

Marshall Field's
111 North State St.
Chicago, IL 60602
312-781-1000
Other stores in 17
Chicago locations as well
as those located in Dallas
and Houston, Tex., and
Wisconsin.
Chrome/leather chairs;
marble dining tables;

Sindbad sofas by Vico Magistretti. Cassina, Italy

lacquer furniture; wood
and decorated furniture
reproductions; decorative
accessories; porcelain;
Christmas ornaments; art
glass. (R)

———

Susan P. Meisel
133 Prince St.
New York, NY 10012
212-254-0137
Furniture by Bugatti,
statues by Chiparus,
Zach, and Preiss. (R)

———

Alan Moss
88 Wooster St.
New York, NY 10012
212-219-1663
Furniture from the Art
Deco period to the 1950s;

furniture by Giò Ponti,
Albini, vintage Italian
glass and glass sculpture.
(R) (W)

———

Lillian Nassau
220 East 57th St.
New York, NY 10022
212-759-6062
Art Nouveau and Art
Deco furniture; ceramics,
sculpture. (R) (W)

———

Nina International
518 Davis St.
Evanston, IL 60201
312-475-2010

4801 Pembroke Rd.
Hollywood, FL 33021
305-961-6155
Dining room, living room,
and bedroom furniture in
high gloss and various
lacquered woods;
Murano glass lamps;
swags. (W)

———

Oggetti
48 Northwest 25th St.

Verona cotton market um-
brella. Pottery Barn, New York

MARIO CARRIERI

Bilama table by Giovanni Offredi. Saporiti International

Miami, FL 33127
305-576-1044
Representatives in
Atlanta, Ga.; Boston,
Mass.; Chicago, Ill.;
Cleveland, Ohio; Dallas
and Houston, Tex.;
Denver, Colo.;
Huntington Beach, San
Diego, San Francisco,
Cal.; Minneapolis, Minn.;
New York City,
Philadelphia, Pa.;
Phoenix, Ariz.; Pittsburgh,
Pa.; Portland, Ore.; Troy,
Mich.; Seattle, Wash.;
Washington, D.C.
Range of decorative
accessories in glass,
porcelain, horn, marble,
and brass; ceramics;
hand-painted porcelain
fish. (W)

The Oggo Corporation
1010 Southwest 32nd
Court
P.O. Box 22149
Fort Lauderdale, FL
33335
305-525-5503
Armchairs, side chairs,
bar stools, and counter

stools in a variety of
finishes, colors, and
coverings. (R) (W)

Oops, Inc.
528 La Guardia Pl.
New York, NY 10012
212-982-0586
Imperfect pieces of
furniture from early 1900s
to present. (R)

The Pace Collection, Inc.
321 East 62nd St.
New York, NY 10021
212-838-0331
Wholesale showrooms in
Atlanta, Ga.; Chicago,
Ill.; Dallas, Tex.; Los
Angeles, Cal.; Miami,
Fla.
Contemporary seating,
tables, desks, cabinets,
and beds; sculptured
glass. (W)

Placewares
351 Congress St.
Boston, MA 02110
617-451-2074
Other retail outlets in

Alexandria, Va., and
Boston, Concord,
Wellesley, Mass.
Shelving and desks
imported from Italy. (R) (MO)

The Pottery Barn
231 10th Ave.
New York, NY 10011
212-741-9120
Other stores in New York
City, Manhasset, and
Scarsdale; Hartford and
Stamford, Conn.
Cotton Verona umbrellas,
flowerpots, summer
furniture. (R)

Prince St. Antiquities Ltd.
106 Prince St.
New York, NY 10012
212-966-7235
Wide selection of Art
Deco furniture. (R) (W)

Rachlin Furniture, Inc.
628 Columbia Ave.
Sinking Spring, PA 19608
215-678-3438
Showrooms in City of
Industry, Cal.; Robesonia,
Pa.; Winnsboro, S.C.
Wood and metal tubular
chairs and tables. (W)

Rapport Co., Inc.
435 North La Brea Ave.
P.O. Box 480590
Los Angeles, CA 90048
213-930-1500
Enormous assortment of
contemporary Italian
furniture. (R)

Riedel Crystal of America
24 Aero Rd.
Bohemia, NY 11716
516-567-7575
Venini colored art glass
from Murano, Italy. (W)

Roche Bobois
200 Madison Ave.
New York, NY 10016
212-725-5513
Contemporary Italian
chairs, tables, sofas,
dining and cocktail
tables. (R)

Don Rose Galleries
751 North Wells
Chicago, IL 60610
312-337-4052
Art Nouveau and Art
Deco furniture; bronzes.
(R) (W)

Campaniello Imports
Saporiti Italia
225 East 57th St.
New York, NY 10022
212-371-3700

Campaniello Imports of
Florida, Inc.
180 N.E. 39th St.
Miami, FL 33137-0249
305-576-9494

Campaniello Imports Ltd.
Dallas Design Center
1025 North Stemmons
Freeway, Suite 100
Dallas, TX 75207
214-747-8303

Campaniello Imports Ltd.
Pacific Design Center
8687 Melrose Ave.
Los Angeles, CA 90069
213-854-0990
Complete line of Saporiti

"Wave" chair by Giovanni Offredi. Saporiti International

International furniture; sofas, chairs, tables, wall units, tapestries, bedroom pieces. (W)

———

Scalia, Inc.
305 East 63rd St.
New York, NY 10021
212-759-3943
Wholesale showrooms in Atlanta, Ga.; Dallas, Tex. Retail stores in Morristown and Paterson, N.J. Busnelli residential and contract furniture lines, custom furniture designs in imported skins; custom period reproductions in wood, painted and faux finishes; lithographs and decorative accessories. (R) (W)

———

Sotheby Parke Bernet, Inc.
1334 York Ave. at 72nd St.
New York, NY 10021
212-606-7000
(For 24-hour auction and exhibition information call 212-606-7245).
Art Nouveau, Art Deco, and other modern furniture from 1890 to 1950.

———

Stendig International, Inc./B & B America/Stendig Textiles
745 Fifth Ave.
New York, NY 10151
212-752-5234
Showrooms in Chicago, Ill.; Dallas, Tex.; Los

Sketch for GAIA chair by Carlo Bartoli. Arflex, Italy

Angeles, Cal.; Miami, Fla.; Washington, D.C.. Sales offices in Boston, Mass.; Milwaukee, Wis.; San Francisco, Cal. Additional representatives and sales offices throughout the United States.
B & B Italia furniture; chairs, tables, wall units, sofas, and beds. (W)

———

Storehouse, Inc.
2737 Apple Valley Rd. N.E.
Atlanta, GA 30319
404-262-2926
Other stores in Atlanta, Ga.; Austin, Dallas, Fort Worth, Houston, San Antonio, Tex; Charlotte and Raleigh, N.C.; Greenville, S.C.; Nashville, Tenn.; New Orleans, La.; Tampa, Fla.; Tulsa, Okla. Modern classic designs by Le Corbusier; Breuer chairs; stacking chairs, desk chairs, and table

bases imported from Italy. (R)

———

Gabriel Victor Custom Furniture Collections
9046 Culver Blvd.
Culver City, CA 90230
213-837-8775
Custom reproductions of a range of Italian period furniture. (R) (W)

———

Maurice Villency, Inc.
200 Madison Ave.
New York, NY 10016
212-725-4840
Retail stores in Paramus, N.J.; Roslyn Heights, Scarsdale, N.Y. Contemporary Italian sofas, tables, beds. (R)

———

MODERN FURNITURE AND OBJECTS IN ITALY

———

Arflex
Via Borgogna 2

20122 Milano
02/705972

Via del Babuino 19
00187 Roma
06/3612221
Upholstered and non-upholstered furniture by Cini Boeri, Carla Venosta, and a group of international designers. (R)

———

B & B Italia
Corsia dei Servi 11
Milano
02/705531
Contemporary upholstered and nonupholstered furniture. (R)

———

Cassina
Via Durini 18
Milano
02/790745

Via del Babuino 100/101
Roma
06/679330
Contemporary Italian furniture by leading Italian designers and reproductions of classics of early modern masters: Le Corbusier, Charles

Rennie Mackintosh, Gerrit Rietveld. (R)

———

Driade
Via Fatebenefratelli 9
Milano
02/657301

at Arcom
Via della Scrofa 104
Roma
06/6568354
Contemporary cabinets, wall units, upholstered sofas, tables and chairs. (R)

———

Kartell
at Selvini
Via C. Poerio 3
Milano
02/706118

at Arcom
Via della Scrofa 104
Roma
06/6568354
High-tech plastic furniture and decorative accessories. (R) (W)

———

Maxalto
at Ambienti
Galleria Passarella 2
Milano
02/780285

Alanda chair by Paolo Piva. B&B, Stendig International

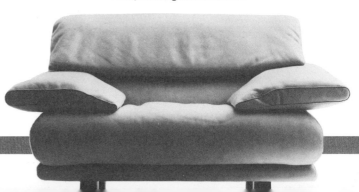

"Kristall" wood and laminate table by Michele de Lucchi. Memphis

Del'Amima 55
Roma
06/6547139
Furniture designed by Gae Aulenti, Achille Castiglioni, De Pas, D'Urbino, Lomazzi, Paolini and Teodoro, Marco Zanuso. **(R)**

AVANT-GARDE

at Ellen B.
Via Cardinal Ginnasi 12
Lido di Ostia, Roma
06/5600854
Contemporary sofas, tables, chairs. **(R)**

Vivai Del Sud
Corso Monforte 16
Milano
02/702690

Via delle Terme di Caracalla
Roma
06/7596796
Contemporary indoor and outdoor furniture; cotton patio umbrellas. **(R)**

Zanotta
at Rosi Riparato
Corso Garibaldi 97-99
Milano
02/6552254

at Spazio 7
Via Santa Maria

Complete line of Memphis furniture. **(W)**

City
213 West Institute Pl.
Chicago, IL 60610
312-664-9581
Memphis furniture. **(R) (MO)**

Furniture of the Twentieth Century
227 West 17th St.
New York, NY 10011
212-929-6023
Furniture designed by Ettore Sottsass, Michele de Lucchi, Matteo Thun. **(W)**

Grace Design
2315 Albans
Houston, TX 77005
713-520-8614

Italiano Displays, Inc.
7980 North French Dr.
Suite 402
Pembroke Pines, FL 33024
305-962-7193
Selection of Italian avant-garde furniture. **(W)**

Janus Gallery
8000 Melrose Ave.
Los Angeles, CA 90069
213-658-6084
Complete line of Memphis furniture. **(W)**

Memphis-Milan
150 East 58th St.
New York, NY 10155
212-980-9313
Complete line of Memphis furniture. **(W)**

Detail of hand-embroidered bed linens. Frette

AVANT-GARDE FURNITURE IN ITALY

Alchimia
Museo Alchimia
Foro Bonaparte 55
Milano
02/861171
Highly allegorical, neomodern furniture. **(R) (W)**

I Luoghi Del XX Secolo
Costa San Giorgio 2/R
Firenze
055/212391
Alchimia tables, chairs, sofas. **(R) (W)**

Memphis
Arc 74 Design Center
Corso Europa 2
Milano
02/798417

Experimental furniture by an international group of architects and designers. **(R) (W)**

FOR BED & BATH

Ad-Hoc Housewares
842 Lexington Ave.
New York, NY 10021
212-752-5489

Ad-Hoc Softwares
410 West Broadway
New York, NY 10010
212-925-2652
Towels and bathroom accessories. **(R) (W) (MO)**

Elements
New York Design Center
200 Lexington Ave.
New York, NY 10016
212-532-9494
Bathroom fixtures imported from Italy. **(W)**

Frette
787 Madison Ave.
New York, NY 10021
212-988-5221
Other stores in Beverly Hills, Cal.; Houston, Tex.; Palm Beach, Fla.; Shaxted, Ill.
Embroidered cotton and linen sheets, towels and bathroom accessories. **(R)**

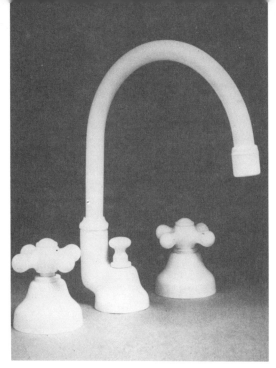

White enamel gooseneck set from the Colore series. Watercolors

Placewares
351 Congress St.
Boston, MA 02210
617-451-2074
Other outlets in
Alexandria, Va.; Boston,
Concord, Wellesley,
Mass.
Towel bars and
bathroom accessories
imported from Italy. (R)

Pratesi
829 Madison Ave.
New York, NY 10021
212-288-2315
Other stores in Bal
Harbour and Beverly
Hills, Cal.; Chicago, Ill.;
Palm Beach, Fla.
Embroidered cotton and
linen sheets, towels, and
bathrobes. (R)

Shaxted & Co.
107 East Oak St.
Chicago, IL 60611
312-337-0855
Bath towels, imported
from Italy. (R)

Watercolors
Garrison-on-Hudson
New York, NY 10524
914-424-3327
Imported modern Italian
bathroom fixtures. (R) (W)

FOR FABRICS AND WALL COVERINGS

Roger Arlington
979 Third Ave.
New York, NY 10022
212-752-5288
Representatives in
Atlanta, Ga.; Boston,
Mass.; Chicago, Ill.;
Denver, Colo.; Dallas
and Houston, Tex.;
Miami, Fla.; Portland,
Ore.; San Francisco,
Cal.; Seattle, Wash.
Luxury woven upholstery
fabrics, printed drapery
fabrics, woven silk
documentary fabrics. (W)

Gretchen Bellinger, Inc.
979 Third Ave.
New York, NY 10022
212-688-2850
Linen chenille, linen
velvet, custom-colored
velvet, iridescent silk, silk
shantung, silk window
and wall coverings, wool
plush fabrics. (R) (W)

Brunschwig & Fils, Inc.
979 Third Ave.
New York, NY 10022
212-838-7878

Showrooms in Atlanta,
Ga.; Boston, Mass.;
Chicago, Ill.; Dallas and
Houston, Tex.; Denver,
Colo.; Laguna Niguel,
Los Angeles, San
Francisco, Cal.; Miami,
Fla.; Philadelphia, Pa.;
Seattle, Wash.
Wide range of woven
textiles, brocades,
damasks, silk, cotton
prints, lampas. (W)

Clarence House
40 East 57th St.
New York, NY 10022
212-752-2890
Showrooms in Atlanta,
Ga.; Boston, Mass.;
Chicago, Ill.; Dallas and
Houston, Tex.; Denver,
Colo.; Miami, Fla.;
Montreal, Can.;
Philadelphia, Pa.;
Portland, Ore.; San
Francisco and Los

Angeles, Cal.; Seattle,
Wash.; Troy, Mich.
Printed cotton, silk
damask, silk, linen
damask, cut velvet,
printed cotton velvet,
brocade fabrics. (W)

Decorators Walk
245 Newtown Rd.
Plainview, NY 11803
516-249-3100
Sales representatives in
Atlanta, Ga.; Boston,
Mass.; Chicago, Ill.;
Dallas and Houston, Tex.;
Denver, Colo.; Miami,
Fla.; Philadelphia, Pa.;
San Francisco and Los
Angeles, Cal.; Seattle,
Wash.; Washington, D.C.
Brocade, brocatelle,
damask, lace, lampas,
lisere, marquisette,
matelass, velvet, woven
tapestry fabric. (W)

Cotton Gobelin weave tapestry depicting Italian countryside. Lovelia Enterprises

Primula porcelain dinnerware. Pottery Barn

Durawall, Inc.
979 Third Ave.
New York, NY 10022
212-355-3888
Showrooms in Atlanta, Ga.; Chicago, Ill.; Dallas and Houston, Tex.; Denver, Colo.; Los Angeles, Cal.; Miami, Fla.; Portland, Ore.; Washington, D.C.
Textile wall coverings. (W)

———

East and Orient Co.
2901 North Henderson Ave.
Dallas, TX 75206
214-826-1191
Italian silk drapery and upholstery fabrics. (R) (W)

———

Fortuny
509 Madison Ave.
New York, NY 10022
212-753-7153
Cotton upholstery fabrics. (R) (W)

Import Guild, Inc./ Old World Weavers
136 East 57th St.
New York, NY 10022
212-355-7186
Cut velvet, damask, lampas, taffeta. (W)

———

Jack Lenor Larsen
232 East 59th St.
New York, NY 10022
212-674-3993

———

41 East 11th St.
New York, NY 10003
(corporate offices)
212-674-3993
Other showrooms in Atlanta, Ga.; Boston, Mass.; Chicago, Ill.; Dallas and Houston, Tex.; Denver, Colo.; Honolulu, Hawaii; Miami, Fla.; Philadelphia, Pa.; Phoenix, Ariz.; Portland, Ore.; San Francisco and Los Angeles, Cal.; Seattle, Wash.
Jacquard corduroy, damask, tapestry, cotton and printed velvets, moire, wool carpets. (W)

Lovelia Enterprises, Inc.
356 East 41st St.
New York, NY 10017
212-490-0930
Aubusson and Gobelin machine-woven tapestries from Italy, France, and Belgium for wall hangings, upholstery fabrics, pillows. (R) (W) (MO)

———

Scalamandré Silks
950 Third Ave.
New York, NY 10022
212-980-3888
Other showrooms in Atlanta, Ga.; Boston, Mass.; Chicago, Ill.; Dallas and Houston, Tex.; Los Angeles and Orange Co., Cal.; Philadelphia, Pa.; Washington, D.C.
Hand-printed silk and cotton, paperbacked wall covering, brocatelle, velvet, hand-cut velvet and jacquard velvets, damask, lisere, lampas, taffeta, twill, trimmings. (W)

———

F O R   K I T C H E N   A N D   T A B L E

———

Singing teakettle designed by Richard Sapper. Alessi

Ad-Hoc Housewares
842 Lexington Ave.
New York, NY 10021
212-752-5489
Bormioli glassware, Alessi flatware, espresso coffee maker and tea-kettle designed by Richard Sapper for Alessi, service plates, cocktail shakers, Paderno cookware. (R) (W) (MO)

———

Ad-Hoc Softwares
410 West Broadway
New York, NY 10010
212-925-2652
Table linens from Telene and Galimbetti. (R) (W) (MO)

———

Alessi USA
The Schawbel Corp.
281 Albany St.
Cambridge, MA 02139
617-492-2100
Teakettles and espresso machines designed by the German architect Richard Sapper, stainless steel serving pieces and baskets, oil/vinegar, salt/pepper sets, bar accessories, and place settings.
At fine stores throughout the USA. (R)

———

The Bridge Co.
214 East 52nd St.
New York, NY 10022

Espresso machine designed by Richard Sapper. Alessi

212-688-4220
Paderno kitchenware. (R)

———

Buccellati, Inc.
46 East 57th St.
New York, NY 10022
212-308-2900
Sterling hollowware and flatware. (R)

———

Trump Tower
725 Fifth Ave.
New York, NY 10022
212-308-6900
Murano glass, Bassani porcelain, and imported candles. (R)

———

Bulgari
Hotel Pierre
2 East 61st St.

New York, NY 10021
212-486-0086
Silver glasses, wine canisters, flatware, bowls, water pitchers; cigarette and cigar cases. **(R)**

City
213 West Institute Pl.
Chicago, IL 60610
312-664-9581
Alessi tableware and flatware. **(R) (MO)**

Oil and vinegar, salt and pepper sets designed by Ettore Sottsass. Alessi

Crate and Barrel
190 Northfield Rd.
Northfield, IL 60093
312-446-9300
Other stores in Boston and Cambridge, Mass.; Chicago, Ill.; Dallas, Tex. Contemporary Italian dinnerware, ceramic bowls, and glass platters; espresso machines. **(R)**

Country Floors, Inc.
300 East 61st St.
New York, NY 10021
212-758-7414
Other stores and

representatives in Atlanta, Ga.; Austin, Dallas, Houston, San Antonio, Tex.; Birmingham, Ala.; Boston, Mass.; Chicago, Ill.; Cleveland and Columbus, Ohio; Denver, Colo.; High Point, N.C.; Los Angeles, Santa Ana, Santa Barbara, Cal.; Memphis, Tenn.; Miami, Fla.; Overland Park, Kan.; Philadelphia and Pittsburgh, Pa.; Portland, Me.; Rutland, Vt.; Troy, Mich.; Tulsa, Okla.; Washington, D.C. Italian hand-painted plates, platters, bowls, vases, cachepots. **(R) (W)**

Dean and DeLuca Imports
110 Greene St.
New York, NY 10012
212-431-1691
800-221-7714 (outside New York State)
Other stores in Atlanta, Ga.; Chicago, Ill.; Dallas, Tex.; Durham, N.C.; San Francisco, Cal.; Seattle, Wash.
Paderno kitchenwear. **(R) (W) (MO)**

Frette
787 Madison Ave.
New York, NY 10021
212-988-5221
Other outlets in Beverly Hills, Cal.; Houston, Tex.;

Venini glass vases. Fifty-50

Palm Springs, Cal.; Shaxted, Ill.
Cotton damask and linen tablecloths and napkins. **(R)**

Kitchen Bazaar
4455 Conn. Ave. N.W.
Washington, DC 20008
202-363-4600
Other stores in Baltimore, Md., and Falls Church, Va. Glassware, vases, and an assortment of kitchen utensils. **(R) (W) (MO)**

Martin of London
8401 Melrose Pl.

Los Angeles, CA 90069
213-653-1566
Italian china exclusive to Martin of London. **(W)**

Museum of Modern Art Bookstore
11 West 53rd St.
New York, NY 10019
212-708-9700
For mail order write

Linen hand-embroidered bedsheets. Frette

CALVIN REDMOND

Atollo lamp by Vico Magistretti. Lighting Associates

Publication Sales
Museum of Modern Art
Bookstore
11 West 53rd St.
New York, NY 10019
Alessi espresso machines,
Brionvega radios, Danese
desk accessories. **(R) (MO)**

___

Pratesi
829 Madison Ave.
New York, NY 10021
212-288-2315
Retail stores in Bal
Harbour and Beverly
Hills, Cal.; Chicago, Ill.;
Palm Beach, Fla.
Embroidered linen and
cotton damask
tablecloths, place mats,
napkins. **(R)**

___

The Pottery Barn
231 Tenth Ave.
New York, NY 10011
212-741-9120
Other stores in Hartford
and Stamford, Conn.;

Manhasset, New York
City, and Scarsdale, N.Y.
Earthenware plates,
bowls, serving pieces,
glassware imported from
Italy. **(R) (MO)**

___

Ricci Silversmiths
41 Madison Ave. #10 A
New York, NY 10010
212-696-9036

5700 West Pico Blvd.
Los Angeles, CA 90019
213-933-5929
Contemporary and
traditional flatware and
hollowware. **(W)**

___

D. F. Sanders and Co.
368 West Broadway
New York, NY 10012
212-334-8080
Alessi flatware,
teakettles, and espresso
machines; Richard
Sagger tea carts; table
linens by Naj-Oleari.

___

Wolfman Gold & Good Co.
484 Broome St.
New York, NY 10013
212-431-1888

142 East 73rd St.
New York, NY 10021
212-288-0404
Glassware, china
platters, hand towels, and
napkins imported from
Italy. **(R)**

F O R   L I G H T I N G

___

Arango
7519 Dadeland Mall
Miami, FL 33156
305-661-4229

___

The Galleria
2384 East Sunrise Blvd.
Fort Lauderdale, FL
33304
305-563-6688
Modern Italian lighting
from Magis, Artek, Sicart,
Sambonet. **(R)**

___

Artemide
150 E. 58th St.
New York, NY 10022
212-980-0710

851 Merchandise Mart
Chicago, IL 60654
312-644-0510

266 Pacific Design Center
8687 Melrose Ave.
Los Angeles, CA 90069
213-659-1708
Clamp-on table, floor

lamps, track lighting,
outdoor garden lamps by
Artemide; the Tizio lamp
by Richard Sapper;
designs by Ernesto
Gismondi, Mario Bellini,
Vico Magistretti. **(W)**

___

Atelier International Ltd.
595 Madison Ave.
New York, NY 10022
212-644-0400

9-100 Merchandise Mart
Chicago, IL 60654
312-329-0360

608 World Trade Center
Dallas, TX 75258
214-653-1161

8687 Melrose Ave.
Los Angeles, CA 90069
213-659-9402

300 D. Street, S.W.
Washington, DC 20024
202-484-1287
For addresses and phone

numbers of additional
sales offices in Boston,
Mass.; Branford, Conn.;
Coral Gables, Fla.;
Denver, Colo.; Seattle,
Wash.—call the New
York office.
Lighting from Flos;
designs by Achille
and Pier Giacomo
Castiglioni. **(W)**

___

Current
815 East Thomas
Seattle, WA 98102
206-325-2995
Lighting from Tronconi,
O-Luce, Luci, Stilnovo,
Dalca, Castaldi, Zerbetto,
Cil, Cini&Nils, Effetre. **(R) (W)**

___

Domus
1214 Perimeter Mall
4400 Ashford Dunwoody Rd.
Atlanta, GA 30346
404-396-1064
Tronconi lighting **(R) (MO)**

Papillona floor lamp by Tobia Scarpa. Atelier International

Fifty-50
793 Broadway
New York, NY 10003
212-777-3208
Italian lighting from the
1940s and 1950s. (R)

**Valigia lamp designed by Et-
tore Sottsass. Stilnovo**

RODOLFO FACCHINI

Sam Flax
55 East 55th St.
New York, NY 10022
212-620-3000
Phone orders:
800-221-9818
(outside New York State)
800-522-7111
(in New York State)
Other stores in Atlanta,
Ga.; Tampa, Fla.;
Woburn, Mass.
Lighting from Artemide.
(R) (MO)

Furniture of the Twentieth
Century
227 West 17th St.
New York, NY 10011

212-929-6023
Early-20th-century lamps
by Mariano Fortuny;
lighting from Bieffe. (W)

Interna Designs Ltd.
Merchandise Mart
6-168
Chicago, IL 60654
312-467-6076
Fontana Arte lighting. (W)

Lighting Associates, Inc.
305 East 63rd St.

New York, NY 10021
212-751-0575
Lighting by O-Luce,
Barbini, and Lumina and
other contemporary
Italian lighting
manufacturers. (W)

Lighting by Kenneth, Inc.
3816 N.E. First Ave.
Miami, FL 33133
305-573-5040
Lighting from
contemporary Italian
manufacturers. (R) (W)

Martin of London
8401 Melrose Pl.
Los Angeles, CA 90069
213-653-1566
Antique lighting fixtures. (W)

Alan Moss
88 Wooster St.
New York, NY 10012
212-219-1663
Art Deco lighting, lamps
from the 1950s. (R) (W)

Museum of Modern Art
Bookstore
11 West 53rd St.
New York, NY 10019
212-708-9700
For mail order write
Publication Sales
Museum of Modern Art
Bookstore
11 West 53rd St.
New York, NY 10019

Artemide and O-Luce
lighting. (R) (MO)

Nina International
518 Davis St.
Evanston, IL 60201
312-475-2010

4801 Pembroke Rd.
Hollywood, FL 33021
305-961-6155
Contemporary Murano
glass lamps. (W)

D. F. Sanders and Co.
386 West Broadway
New York, NY 10012
212-334-8080
Lighting from Artemide. (R)

Scalia, Inc.
305 East 63rd St.
New York, NY 10021
212-759-3943
Wholesale showrooms in
Atlanta, Ga.; Dallas,
Tex.; retail stores in Morris-
town and Paterson, N.J.
Range of contemporary
Italian lighting fixtures.
(R) (W)

Thunder 'n Light, Inc.
171 Bowery
New York, NY 10002
212-219-0180
Lighting by Stilnovo,
Altalite, Targetti,
Structura, Controluce.
(R) (W)

**Taccia lamp by Achille and Pier
Giacomo Castiglioni. Atelier
International**

L I G H T I N G
I N   I T A L Y

Arteluce
at Bozzola
Corso Monforte 9
Milano
02/701641

Arteluce
at Crimaldi
Via del Babuino 84
Roma
02/6795978
Table, wall, floor lamps
by contemporary Italian
designers. (R)

Artemide
Corso Monforte 19
Milano
02/706930

Artemide
Via Margutta 107
Roma
02/6784917
Lighting fixtures by Cini
Boeri, Mario Bellini, Vico
Magistretti, Gae Aulenti,
and Livio Castiglioni. (R)

Flos
Via del Babuino 6
Roma
06/6795978

Flos
Corso Monforte 9
Milano
02/701641
Dramatic contemporary
lighting designed by the
Castiglioni brothers and
Tobia Scarpa. (R)

O-Luce
Via Borgonuovo 1
Milano
02/800907
Range of lamps designed
by Vico Magistretti,
Marco Zanuso, and Joe
Colombo. (R)

Stilnovo
Via Turati 3
Milano
02/6555957

Stilnovo
Via Due Macelli 32
Roma
06/6793772
Table, floor, wall and
ceiling lamps designed
by Joe Colombo, Ettore
Sottsass, Gae Aulenti,
and Livio Castiglioni. (R)

FOR SPECIAL EFFECTS

Architectural Sculpture
242 Lafayette St.
New York, NY 10012
212-431-5873
Architectural ornaments;
capitals, corbels,
pedestals, neoclassic
moldings, ceiling
medallions, bas-reliefs. (R)
(MO) and by commission.

Full Moonworks, Inc.
110 Greene St. Suite 706
New York, NY 10012
212-334-9636
Hand-carved wood
moldings, wainscoting,
baseboards. (R)

Great American Salvage Co.
34 Cooper Square
New York, NY 10003
212-505-0700
Classical columns, urns. (R)

Hudson Paper Tube Co.
80 Furler St.
Totowa, NJ 07511
212-226-3858, -3759
Nonstructural columns in
cardboard available
from diameters of one to
16 inches. (R)

Irreplaceable Artifacts
259 Bowery
New York, NY 10012
212-982-5000

**Corinthian capital in reinforced plaster.
Architectural Sculpture**

14 Second Ave.
New York, NY 10003
212-777-2900
Architectural elements
from the 1700s to the
1920s. Columns, corbels,
gargoyles in terra-cotta,
marble, wood. Wrought-
and cast-iron gates,
grilles. (R) (W)

Let There Be Neon
510 Broadway
New York, NY 10013
212-966-4772
Neon signs and
decorative pieces.
Custom work to architects
exclusively.

Old World Molding and
Finishing
115 Allen Blvd.
Farmingdale, NY 11735

516-293-1789
Machine-carved molding
in ash, cherry, pine,
mahogany, and oak.
Chair rail, baseboard,
panel and trim moldings.
(R) (MO)

Saldarini and Pucci
196 4th Ave.
Brooklyn, NY 11217
718-852-1656
Wooden columns; plaster
corbels, capitals,
cornices, ceiling pieces. (R)

Special Wall Treatments
David Cohn
212-741-3548
Floor and wall stenciling,
trompe l'oeil, wallpaper
effects, decorative
glazes. By commission
only.

**Roman "Campana Relief":
Flying Victory or Nike Holding
Wreath and Palm. Late first-
early second century A.D.
Royal Athena Galleries**

Christian Thee
39 Columbia Pl.
Brooklyn Heights, NY
11201
718-834-1513
Murals, trompe l'oeil,
and scenic environments.
By commission only.

———

Tromploy
400 Lafayette St.
New York, NY 10003
212-420-1639

columns, and gargoyles.
(R) (W) (MO)

———

Joseph Young
Art in Architecture
7917½ W. Norton Ave.
Los Angeles, CA 90046
213-656-2286, 654-0990

New York, NY 10022
212-832-8193
Ceramic, terra-cotta,
glazed and unglazed tiles
in solid and decorative
patterns. (W)

**Commissioned trompe l'oeil
murals painted on canvas.
Tromploy, New York**

Trompe l'oeil wall
treatments, interior and
exterior murals, faux
marble floors, illusionary
and decorative ceilings,
painted folding screens.
By commission.

———

Urban Archaeology
135 Spring St.
New York, NY 10012
212-431-6969
Architectural ornaments,

Italian mosaic murals,
bas-reliefs, tapestries,
stained glass, three-
dimensional works in
marble, granite, bronze,
cast concrete.
By commission only.

———

FOR WALL AND
FLOOR TILES

———

Agency Tile
D&D Building
979 Third Ave.

Amaru Tile
D&D Building
979 Third Ave.
New York, NY 10022
212-750-8804
Wall and floor tiles,
outdoor tiles, terra-cotta,
glazed and unglazed
tiles. (W)

———

Benson Tiles
1748 86th St.
Brooklyn, NY 11214
718-837-3500
Tiles designed by Laura
Biagiotti. (W)

Ceramica Mia
405 East 51st St.
New York, NY 10022
212-759-2339
Floor, wall, hand-
painted, and designer
tiles. (R)

**Glazed ceramic Italian tiles by
Cernova. Parma Tile**

City-Tile
435 West 46th St.
New York, NY 10036
212-664-0297
Ceramic tiles in white,
gray and earth tones,
white Carrara, Breccian
marble. (R)

———

Country Floors, Inc.
300 East 61st St.

Modern kitchen bed and bath tiles. Agency Tile, Amaru Tile, Hastings Tile, Parma Tile, and Rico Tile

New York, NY 10021
212-758-7414

8735 Melrose Ave.
Los Angeles, CA 90069
213-657-0510
Other stores and representatives in Atlanta, Ga.; Austin, Dallas, Houston, San Antonio, Tex.; Birmingham, Ala.; Boston, Mass.; Chicago, Ill.; Cleveland and Columbus, Ohio; Denver, Colo.; High Point, N.C.; Memphis, Tenn.; Miami, Fla.; Overland Park, Kan.; Philadelphia and Pittsburgh, Pa.; Portland, Me.; Rutland, Vt.; St. Louis, Mo.; Troy, Mich.; Tulsa, Okla.; Washington, D.C. Italian terra-cotta tiles, hand-painted ceramic tiles. (R) (W)

Hastings Tile
201 East 57th St.
New York, NY 10022
212-755-2710
Glazed decorative floor and wall tiles. (R) (W)

Integrity Tile Co.
The Marketplace
2400 Market St.
Philadelphia, PA 19103
215-567-9025
Ceramic and marble tiles. (R) (W)

Marazzi USA, Inc.
950 Third Ave.
New York, NY 10022
212-888-7391
Matte and glazed floor and wall tiles. (W)

Maxsam
2 Claire Rd.
East Brunswick, NJ 08816
201-238-4411
Tiles designed by Gae Aulenti for Iris Ceramica. (R)

Monarch Tile Manufacturing, Inc.
P.O. Box 2401
San Angelo, TX 76902
915-655-9193
Stores and showrooms in Anaheim, Bakersfield, Newbury Park, San Diego, Cal.; Denver and Fort Collins, Colo.; Earth City, Mo.; Jacksonville, Fla.; Las Vegas, Nev.; Memphis, Tenn.; Milwaukee, Wis.; Oklahoma City and Tulsa, Okla.; Phoenix and Tucson, Ariz.
Wide assortment of ceramic floor tiles. (R) (W)

Parma Tile
241 East 58th St.
New York, NY 10022
212-751-9393
Glazed decorative floor and wall tiles. (R) (W)

Rico Tile
979 Third Ave.
New York, NY 10022
212-755-6590
Glazed decorative floor and wall tiles. (R) (W)

Shelly Tile Ltd.
979 Third Ave.
New York, NY 10022
212-832-2255
Terra-cotta, glazed and unglazed, floor, wall, and bathroom tiles. (W)

Sunray Ceramics
1507 Rand Rd.
Des Plaines, IL 60016
312-822-9400
Ceramic floor tiles. (W)

Hand-painted tiles by Gabbianelli. Hastings Tile